Regulatory Policy and Behavioural Economics

By Pete Lunn

OECD
BETTER POLICIES FOR BETTER LIVES

Please cite this publication as:
Lunn, P. (2014), *Regulatory Policy and Behavioural Economics*, OECD Publishing.
http://dx.doi.org/10.1787/9789264207851-en

ISBN 978-92-64-20784-4 (print)
ISBN 978-92-64-20785-1 (PDF)

The statistical data for Israel are supplied by and under the responsibility of the relevant Israeli authorities. The use of such data by the OECD is without prejudice to the status of the Golan Heights, East Jerusalem and Israeli settlements in the West Bank under the terms of international law.

Photo credits: Cover © Sergey Nivens – Fotolia.com, © MR.LIGHTMAN – Fotolia.com.

Corrigenda to OECD publications may be found on line at: *www.oecd.org/publishing/corrigenda*.

Foreword

The use of behavioural economics in the design and delivery of regulation is at the forefront of regulatory policy and governance. This approach aims to improve outcomes without using traditional command and control mechanisms by understanding the way that citizens and businesses actually behave rather than how traditional economics assumes that they behave. This publication explores how governments are currently applying behavioural science to design and deliver better regulation.

This publication has been produced under the programme of work of the OECD Regulatory Policy Committee on innovative and effective approaches to regulatory design and management. The OECD Regulatory Policy Division in the Public Governance and Territorial Development Directorate commissioned and provided input and guidance throughout the development of the publication. The OECD Regulatory Policy Division is grateful to the author for fulfilling the unique brief of capturing the latest and current developments in a frontier discipline.

This publication was presented by the author, Dr. Pete Lunn, and approved for publication at the 9th meeting of the Regulatory Policy Committee (RPC) on 13th November 2013.

For more information about this publication please contact Faisal Naru (faisal.naru@oecd.org), Senior Economic Advisor, OECD Regulatory Policy Division.

Acknowledgements

This report is unusual in the extent to which it relies on unpublished material, the documentation of governments and states agencies, and personal communications with experts and policy makers. Consequently, I owe debts of gratitude to a number of individuals that go beyond the normal acknowledgement of colleagues and fellow researchers who have read and commented on drafts. Ideas, tips and examples were mentioned and provided by many people who responded enthusiastically to the idea of pulling together an international account of how behavioural economics is informing policy. Warm thanks are extended to Monica Andersen, Carl Magnus Berglund, Pelle Guldborg Hansen, Olof Johansson-Stenman, Radboud Koning, Håkan Nyman, Andreas Ortmann, Robert Östling, Carsten Smidt, Réné van Bavel and Arnstein Vestre. I am particularly grateful to Liam Delaney, Ian McAuley and Maurice Stucke for offering ideas, papers, extensive discussions and detailed readings of drafts. Thanks also to Jason Somerville and Dane Buchanan for help with drafts. I am very grateful to Faisal Naru for support and insightful comments and to Nick Malyshev of the OECD Regulatory Policy Division for the debate and discussion that initially prompted this review. This report was prepared for publication by Jennifer Stein, who I also thank. Despite these many forms of assistance, any mistakes and omissions are my own.

Table of contents

Figures

Acronyms and abbreviations

CARD Act	Credit Card Accountability Responsibility and Disclosure Act
CFPB	Consumer Financial Protection Bureau
FAFSA	Free Application for Federal Student Aid
FCA	Financial Conduct Authority
HMCTS	Her Majesty's Courts and Tribunal Service
JRC	Joint Research Centre
MCOB	Mortgage Conduct of Business
MPG	Miles-per-gallon
OFGEM	Office of Gas and Electricity Markets
OFT	Office of Fair Trading
OIRA	Office of Information and Regulatory Affairs
RCT	Randomised Controlled Trial
RPC	Regulatory Policy Committee
UKBIT	Behavioural Insights Team at the UK Cabinet Office

Executive summary

In recent years, researchers in behavioural economics and related disciplines have discovered numerous systematic influences on people's economic decisions, many of which run counter to orthodox microeconomics. This report presents an international review of how this relatively new science is being applied to policy, concentrating primarily but not exclusively on regulatory policy. It refers to more than 60 instances of policies that are informed by behavioural economics. It then considers possible lessons for regulatory design and delivery.

Behavioural economics is not straightforward to define, but has its origins in the relationship between psychology and economics – in particular the use of methods imported from experimental psychology. Behavioural economists use repeated experiment and observation to derive principles of economic behaviour. This *inductive* approach contrasts with the traditional *deductive* approach to economics, which deduces theories based on assumptions about what constitutes rational behaviour.

It is important to recognise that behavioural economics and so-called "nudges" are distinct. The former is a scientific subdiscipline; the latter is a particular way to apply its findings to policy, which holds that policy makers should avoid regulations that limit choice (bans, caps, etc.) but can use behavioural science to direct people towards better choices.

Behavioural economics is influencing policy in a number of OECD countries, but most explicitly in the United States and the United Kingdom. An example is the Credit Card Accountability Responsibility and Disclosure Act (CARD Act), which was passed into US law in 2009. The tighter regulation of credit card suppliers introduced in the Act was partly based on behavioural evidence showing how consumers were failing to realise the true cost of credit. Certain types of fees were banned and companies were mandated to provide helpful calculations on bills. Early indications are that the Act may have increased consumer surplus. Many other behaviourally informed initiatives in the United States surround simplifying and standardising consumer information, often as an alternative to stronger regulation.

The UK government has recruited a Behavioural Insights Team (UKBIT), which acts like an internal consultancy for UK policy makers. UKBIT takes an empirical approach, using local policy trials and experiments to test behaviourally informed ideas. Some interventions have been successful in the areas of public health, employment activation, tax evasion, fine recovery, consumer policy, energy conservation and charitable giving. The results often prove surprising – an endorsement of the inductive, empirical approach to policy design.

In other countries, the application of behavioural economics to policy is increasingly common in certain policy areas, especially pensions, tax and consumer protection. The European Commission has engaged in several behaviourally informed initiatives, perhaps most notably the ban in the EU Consumer Rights Directive of pre-ticked boxes in online sales, based on evidence that default settings can have powerful influences on choices.

Most cases where behavioural economics has been applied to policy concern regulatory policy or, frequently, an attempt to pursue regulatory goals without resorting to additional rules or sanctions. An example is tax compliance, where experimental trials show that non-compliance can be reduced by changing the nature or wording of communications with those who fail to file tax returns on time. Behavioural economics has also made inroads in consumer policy, especially in markets with relatively complex products, such as financial services, health insurance and other markets involving service contracts.

Three principles of behavioural economics feature strongly in the early applications to regulatory design. First, choices are influenced by the simplicity of information and of the range of available options. Second, people are drawn towards more convenient options, especially default options. Third, the salience of options or attributes can affect how they are weighted in decisions.

Mandated disclosure of simplified product information is increasingly common, especially in consumer financial services. In some cases regulators seek to simplify the range of products on offer too. These policies are intuitively appealing and may prove popular with consumers. Yet while there is evidence that complexity is causing consumer detriment in some markets, evidence for the success of regulations designed to simplify choice is presently mixed. This suggests that proposed disclosure requirements might benefit from market-specific pre-testing in experiments or, better still, controlled trials, to ensure that the benefits outweigh any additional costs imposed. Incorporating such methods from behavioural economics can therefore complement cost-benefit analyses and regulatory impact assessments.

Decision processes matter too. How people respond to the convenience of options, including whether they are the presented as the default option is attracting the attention of policy makers. This research has strongly influenced the regulation of pensions in a number of countries, but it is expanding into other policy areas, especially where decision makers must balance immediate costs against longer-term benefits.

Regulators can potentially use the fact that choices are influenced by the salience of information to alter the effectiveness of official warnings, advice, etc. But perhaps the greater application of research on salience to policy concerns the possibility that companies will use pricing strategies or product descriptions that make costs or relevant consumer information non-salient. Good regulatory design may be able to limit such behaviours. Yet it is often difficult for policy makers to be sure that consumers' decisions after an intervention are better than before. Again, market-specific evidence may be required.

In some cases research has identified clear decision-making errors, such as failure to take account of non-linearity (e.g. compound interest) in decisions. Regulations can be designed in ways that may counteract these phenomena, aiming to "debias" decision makers. However, identifying an unambiguous improvement in decisions is frequently difficult.

Looking across these early applications of behavioural economics to regulatory design, it is apparent that it is much easier to identify behavioural problems and to devise potential solutions than it is to judge or to measure the associated impacts. This means that behaviourally informed policies to date have concentrated on interventions that are relatively uncontroversial and likely to be popular – decision makers tend to welcome simplification, convenience and the highlighting of important factors, even if they may not appreciate the costs of the policy. But there are other areas where behavioural economic findings suggest the possibility that individuals make substantial costly errors, including when gambling, trading in financial markets, purchasing insurance, or engaging in behaviours with long-term health consequences. Orthodox microeconomics may be unreliable for modelling these decisions, which involve uncertainty and/or long time horizons. The possibility of substantial detriment coupled with the difficulty of determining the size of such effects implies a need for more research and for regulatory design to take an empirical approach that generates evidence specific to the context.

Although the use of behavioural economics in regulatory delivery is less advanced than in regulatory design, the same principles can be applied. Regulations that are simple and convenient to comply with are likely to be more effective. What evidence there is supports this view. Behavioural economics also offers methodologies for testing the effectiveness of regulations, including those in the existing regulatory stock. Behavioural evidence also suggests that regulatory regimes that are perceived as fair and applied evenly are likely to achieve greater degrees of compliance. Regulators therefore need to build and to prize trust.

The present review necessarily concentrates on *explicit* applications of behavioural economic findings. It is therefore important to note that much of the influence of behavioural economics on policy may be *implicit*. Among others, Australia, France, Denmark, Sweden, Norway, the United Kingdom, the United States and the European Commission have identifiable initiatives that aim to promote awareness of behavioural economics among policy makers generally.

Economic regulators in several countries have also begun to recruit behavioural economists to assist with regulatory delivery, particularly in the context of market studies aimed at ensuring consumer protection and effective competition. In several cases these initiatives have resulted in a more empirical approach to regulatory policy, incorporating not just the findings but also the methods of behavioural economics. Behaviourally informed interventions often aim to assist rather than to prohibit certain decisions, in keeping with the idea of regulatory policy as an enabler and facilitator to achieve positive outcomes.

From the position of a sometimes marginalised subdiscipline, behavioural economics has been swept into the mainstream with surprising speed. Most examples of behaviourally informed policies have arisen within the last five years. The spread of behavioural economics in policy making has therefore been rapid, wide and, on the evidence surveyed in this review, likely to continue.

1. Introduction

The past several decades have seen great strides made in our understanding of how individuals make economic decisions. Researchers in behavioural economics and related disciplines have discovered and recorded numerous systematic decision-making phenomena, mostly through the use of laboratory and field experiments in which subjects' choices are observed in controlled environments. This work has documented how people's choices vary systematically according to specific aspects of the decisions they face and of the contexts in which their decisions are made. These scientific results have the capacity to improve the ability of researchers and policy makers to predict outcomes when economic actors face different types of decisions in different contexts.

This report presents a review of the application of behavioural economics to policy, concentrating on regulatory policy. The attention paid by policy makers to behavioural economics has increased sharply over the past five years. This review describes the first explicit applications of behavioural economics to policy, most notably in the United States and the United Kingdom, but also to a lesser degree elsewhere. It discusses the extent to which behavioural economics has penetrated the world of the policy maker, drawing attention to policy challenges and potential policy options, as well as resulting in new policies, policy changes or prospective policies under active consideration. It then offers frameworks for understanding these applications of behavioural economics and identifies some emerging themes in the relationship between this relatively young science and public policy. Potential implications for regulatory design and delivery are then considered.

Given, first, that behavioural economics uncovers systematic influences on economic decision making and, second, that regulatory policy concerns how governments and public authorities use rules to influence the behaviour of economic actors, it would be surprising if the relevant scientific advances did not have important implications for policy. The empirical findings of behavioural economics are frequently suggestive as to when a regulation is more or less likely to achieve a particular regulatory goal, because regulations partly determine the context in which economic actors operate.

One important area of study which, although partly unavoidable, is not considered in detail here is the debate surrounding the normative implications of behavioural economics. That is, the present review primarily confines itself to a positive analysis: how is behavioural economics being applied to policy and what inferences might we draw from that? It avoids asking whether authorities have any business trying to influence the decisions of the citizens in whose name they act. Much ink continues to be spilled over whether behavioural economics justifies a more paternalistic approach to policy making; less ink flows into descriptions of how behavioural economics is, in fact, changing policy making. The latter is the aim here.

A notable aspect of the empirical phenomena unearthed by behavioural economics is how regularly they contradict the behaviours predicted by rational choice theory, which holds that individuals adhere to a specific set of choice axioms and make decisions in their own best interests. Rational choice theory forms the basis of orthodox (neoclassical) microeconomics and has underpinned the dominant theoretical approach to the study of economic policy problems over a number of decades. Consequently, the ultimate implications of behavioural economics for policy could turn out to be substantial. Many existing regulations in areas such as competition and consumer policy are, if not inspired by the orthodox approach, at least designed to be consistent with it. Although much debate still surrounds the extent to which rational choice theory and the models it inspired are rendered inaccurate by behavioural phenomena, it is clear at this stage that researchers and policy makers need to take the impact of such phenomena seriously (Garcés, 2010; Micklitz et al., 2011).

Policy makers in several countries are already doing so. Some recent regulatory policies have been designed to be consistent with or to exploit various phenomena identified by behavioural economics. Interventions thus far have mostly concentrated on how simply information is presented to economic actors, the convenience of the different options facing them, the salience of key pieces of information and, to a lesser extent, what actors know about the decisions taken by others. The present review documents and examines these pioneering policies, and also considers why these particular types of interventions have led the way. Box 1 describes two initial examples by way of illustration.

Box 1. Two initial examples of behaviourally informed regulatory policies

EU ban on pre-ticked boxes for online purchases

A substantial amount of evidence shows that decision makers are drawn towards default options. Smith, Goldstein and Johnson (2009) provide an extensive overview of this evidence and a range of examples. Orthodox microeconomics predicts that decisions should not be sensitive to a change in default option, because the optimal option for the decision maker remains unaffected; behavioural economics has shown otherwise. The strength of this effect means that it is possible for suppliers to influence the decisions of consumers by manipulating which option is presented as the default. The default may be signalled with respect to which product is chosen from a range, or which add-on components are to be added to (or taken away from) a basic product specification. This selling tactic may be particularly effective for online purchases, where it is possible to set the default by pre-ticking a box and requiring the purchaser to untick it, or to tick a different box, to avoid purchasing the higher specification product or additional feature. Examples include defaulting consumers into travel insurance when they buy airline tickets, into meals when they purchase accommodation, or into more expensive delivery options when shopping online for consumer goods.

This evidence has directly informed new consumer protection legislation in the European Union. The latest EU Consumer Rights Directive, which is due to be transposed by the end of 2013 and enforced from mid-2014, bans the use of pre-ticked boxes for online sales. Further examples of policies informed by research on defaults are given in Subsections 3.1, 3.2 and 4.2.

US fuel economy labels

Since it is not possible for consumers to observe the fuel economy of a vehicle directly, regulations are employed in many countries that stipulate the use of a standard measure to allow consumers to make comparisons. The standard measure adopted often expresses fuel economy in terms of distance per unit of fuel (e.g. "miles per gallon", "kilometres per litre"). However, the now widely cited study of Larrick and Soll (2008) shows how the non-linearity of such measures induces a "cognitive illusion" that can affect judgements. Ultimately, the cost of running a vehicle depends on how much fuel it requires to travel a given distance. As Figure 1 shows, a difference of 5 miles per gallon has a much larger impact on cost when it is the difference between 10 and 15 miles per gallon than when it is the difference between 50 and 55 miles per gallon. If consumers fail to appreciate this non-linearity, as the evidence provided by Larrick and Soll suggests is likely, they may underinvest in more efficient vehicles.

Box 1. Two initial examples of behaviourally informed regulatory policies (*cont.*)

Recognising the possible implications of this behavioural evidence, the US Environmental Protection Agency changed the regulations covering the labelling of cars. The new regulations require that labels also describe the fuel economy of vehicles in terms of gallons per 100 miles and an estimated annual fuel cost, both of which are linear measures of fuel economy. This is an example where regulation is used in an attempt to "debias" decision makers, after behavioural evidence has identified a potentially negative influence on judgement (see Subsection 4.4). It is worth noting, however, that some recent evidence suggests the impact of this negative influence on actual purchasing behaviour may in any case turn out to be small (Allcott, 2013).

Figure 1. Non-linear relationship between the miles per gallon (MPG) measure and the amount of fuel a vehicle consumes when travelling a given distance

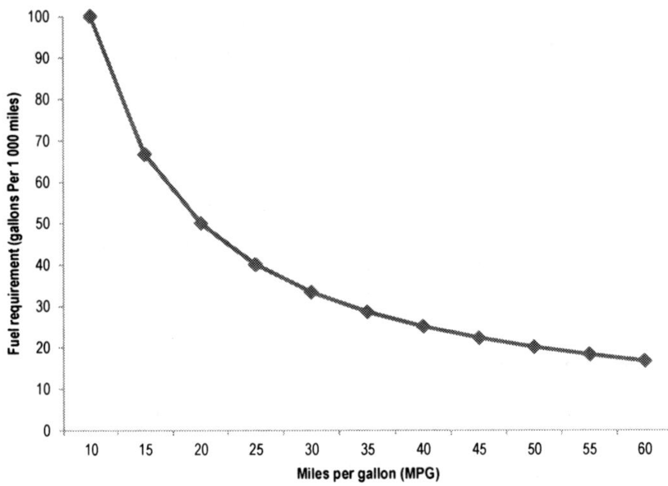

While regulatory policy appears to be an area where behavioural economics has particular relevance, there are other policy areas where it is having an influence. The present review offers a brief stock take on the more general relationship between behavioural economics and policy, since some of the lessons that might be learned from its use in these policy areas may also assist in the design and delivery of regulatory policy.

Regulatory policy is an area that has itself evolved considerably in recent times, regardless of the influence of behavioural economics. There has been a growing acknowledgement that sound regulatory frameworks are important to the creation of efficient and fair markets for firms and consumers, and to the promotion of an economic climate conducive to trade and investment. Many national governments and supranational bodies have undertaken initiatives aimed at regulatory reform, to embed good regulatory practices or to achieve better or smart regulation, driven by recognition that effective regulatory policy is important if the economy is to function smoothly and if opportunities for economic growth are to be realised fully.

The global financial crisis has added urgency to the quest for better regulation. The crisis exposed major failings, not least because regulators placed excessive faith in the efficiency of markets and the ability of actors in financial markets in particular to make sound decisions. The OECD (2012) has published a *Recommendation of the Council on Regulatory Policy and Governance* designed to address some of these failings through a set of recommended principles for high quality regulation. References to these principles and how they relate to behavioural economic findings are made at various points in this report.

It is important to understand that these are early days in the adoption and utilisation of behavioural economics by policy makers. The interface between this science and public policy is a dynamic one, where mistakes are likely to be made and, hopefully, learned from. Trial and error are involved. Early successes of behaviourally inspired policies do not necessarily imply continued success; failures should not be generalised to the view that behavioural economics is just the latest policy fad.

The analysis that follows aims to be thorough, but it is not possible to produce an exhaustive account of how behavioural economics is influencing policy. In part, this reflects the straightforward fact that documenting all instances where regulatory policy is informed by behavioural economics is a task well beyond the scope of this review. Furthermore, instances where behavioural research has provided the central rationale for an intervention are easier to identify than instances where the decision of policy makers has been merely influenced. Yet the latter application of behavioural economics may be common; the behavioural economic perspective on a given policy problem is often just one influence among several. In other cases, the influence of behavioural economics may be hard to identify because it leads to a policy option not being pursued. An example might be mandating the provision of additional product information in a particular market, which ought in theory to benefit an actor behaving according to rational choice theory, but which behavioural economics might suggest is unlikely to be beneficial on the grounds that the available product information is already too complex for consumers to utilise it effectively. An instance such as this, where behavioural insights limit the amount of new regulation, is less likely to be documented than one that results in a new intervention.

Given the above, this review is unavoidably biased towards larger and more prominent examples of where policies are motivated by behavioural evidence. However, the more general influence of behavioural economic concepts should not be underestimated. While compiling this review, the author discussed the application of behavioural economics to policy with experts and policy makers in a range of countries. Many commented that the more general influence of behavioural economic principles and concepts on a broad range of decisions was at least as important as specific policies inspired by behavioural findings.

Undoubtedly, the earliest and most enthusiastic adopters of policies based on behavioural economics are the United States and the United Kingdom. Consequently, applications in these countries account for the lion's share of the examples discussed. These developments are closely associated with a particular approach to the question of how behavioural economics should be applied by policy makers, technically referred to as "libertarian paternalism" but more commonly known as "nudge" (Thaler and Sunstein, 2003, 2008). The central idea of this approach is for authorities to influence the choices of economic actors without constraining those choices. It is important to understand that this approach is only one among a number of possible ways to employ behavioural economics in the design of policy (see Subsection 2.3).

Many of the relevant developments thus far are prospective: policy trials, policy experiments, or behavioural research undertaken in specific policy contexts. To date, there are few regulatory policies that are explicitly based on behavioural economic findings and have stood the test of time or, better still, been properly evaluated following implementation. Yet there are commonalities to the early attempts by regulatory policy makers to exploit behavioural economics, which this review highlights and discusses. Furthermore, there are already signs that policy makers are learning lessons as they go along, both about particular policies and about how best to integrate behavioural economics into regulatory policy.

Since the purpose of this report is to provide a review, it does not as such have a central thesis. Yet it does have a dominant theme. Arguably, current developments suggest that the influence of behavioural economics on regulatory policy relates as much to methods of policy development as to specific interventions undertaken. More specifically, several countries are adopting a more empirical approach, integrating experimentation and controlled trials into the process of regulatory design and aspects of regulatory delivery. This is in keeping with the advance of behavioural economics itself, which has not only brought to economics new findings but also an alternative scientific method.

2. Definitions and scope

2.1 What is behavioural economics?

This question is surprisingly hard to answer, because there is no agreed definition of behavioural economics. All definitions rest to some extent on the relationship between economics and psychology. A standard dictionary definition would be that behavioural economics is the incorporation of psychological insights into the study of economic problems. Some (e.g. Thaler and Mullainathan, 2000) go further in defining behavioural economics more specifically in relation to psychological phenomena that violate aspects of rational choice theory.

In addition to insights from psychology, however, behavioural economics has also incorporated methods (Shiller, 2005). During the twentieth century, experimental psychology emerged as a predominantly inductive science. In other words, findings, principles and theories were derived from repeated observation of behaviour, usually in controlled experiments which systematically manipulated the environment surrounding humans and animals. This primarily inductive scientific method stands in marked contrast to the more deductive method of neoclassical economics, in which theory is mostly deduced from axiomatic assumptions and only then subjected to empirical test. This methodological difference regarding the balance between inductive and deductive reasoning has two implications for how we conceive of behavioural economics. First, inductive experimentation can in principle (and sometimes does) confirm predictions of rational choice theory, so defining behavioural economics as oppositional to rational choice theory is not appropriate. Second, because behavioural economics emphasises behaviour in markets, many of the experimental designs and empirical findings are new to both economics and psychology. That is, psychology may inform behavioural economics, but the converse occurs too. These two implications necessitate a broader definition of behavioural economics (Lunn, 2012).

A further complication is the presence of overlaps between behavioural economics and other fields, including economic psychology, cognitive psychology, decision science, neuroeconomics, marketing science and behavioural science more generally. It is noteworthy that these related disciplines also primarily, though not exclusively, employ inductive scientific approaches. Where the results are relevant to the sorts of economic questions addressed here, it is overwhelmingly because of the possibility that an observed empirical phenomenon generalises to economic and/or regulatory contexts.

Following the above line of argument, the definition of behavioural economics adopted in the context of this review needs to be broad. Behavioural economics is defined here as the application of the inductive scientific method to the study of economic activity. Thus, where empirical studies of decision making and models derived from them are applied to economic problems, this counts as behavioural economics, whether the relevant research is conducted by economists or non-economists of whatever stripe. For present purposes, this definition has the advantage that it casts the net wide when considering the influence of behavioural economics on policy making, which is appropriate for providing an overview. It has the disadvantage that it claims for behavioural economics phenomena that researchers in other disciplines understandably think should be credited to non-economists (cf. Kahneman, 2013).

At this stage, the number of relevant behavioural phenomena that fall under this definition is far too substantial to summarise in this review. The economic decisions of individuals (and to some extent firms) display a large range of systematic relationships between choices made and different properties of the decision structure, perceptions of that structure by the actors, and contexts in which decisions are made. Many findings directly contravene rational choice theory. Very broadly speaking, this occurs in one of two ways. First, results show that people's choices are not consistent, because they vary systematically with, among other things, when decisions are made, how different factors in the decision are presented to decisions-makers, how decision makers must communicate the decision, apparent misperceptions of relevant factors, complexity of the set of choices, and initial endowments. Where choices are inconsistent the implication is that at least some are not optimal. Second, results reveal that people's decisions are based on more than their own outcomes. Most people are concerned about allocative fairness, procedural fairness, trust and reciprocation, while at least some people behave altruistically some of the time. There are many alternative categorisations of the phenomena unearthed by behavioural economics that go beyond this broad two-way classification. High-quality reviews from differing perspectives include: Kahneman (2011), DellaVigna (2009) and Rabin (1998) regarding individual behaviour; Congdon et al. (2011), Sunstein (2011), Dolan et al. (2010) and the recent volume edited by Shafir (2013) in the context of policy making; and Armstrong and Huck (2010) with reference to the decision making of firms.

2.2 *What is regulatory policy?*

It is similarly helpful to adopt a holistic definition of regulatory policy. A standard definition might be the implementation of rules by government and designated authorities to influence the behaviour of private actors in the economy. This definition does not leave room, however, for other forms of intervention that constitute alternatives to rules.

Figure 2. The regulatory cycle

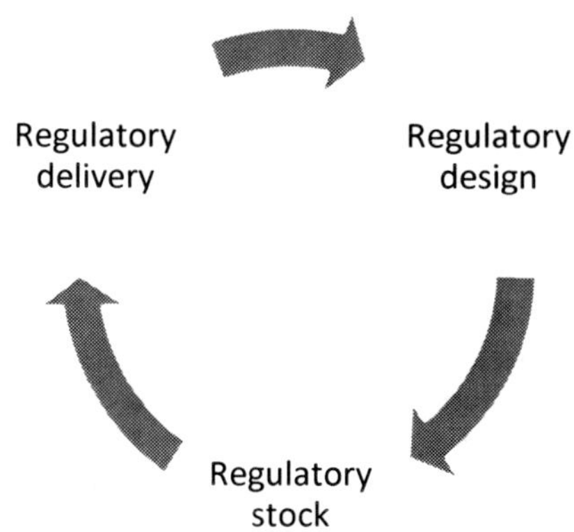

OECD (2012) recognises regulatory policy as the core principles, systems and processes involved in the design, management of the stock and delivery of regulatory quality (Figure 2). One of the early contributions of behavioural economics to regulatory policy has been to support possible ways to obtain regulatory outcomes that do not involve rules, i.e. non-regulatory alternatives designed to achieve the same public policy objectives. It is not a contradiction to regulate through means other than a regulation. A high quality regulatory policy might stress the search for alternatives and regulatory policy might benefit from the evaluation of regulations and the removal of those that do not achieve regulatory goals (OECD, 2012, Recommendations 4 and 5).

In the present context, therefore, regulatory policy is also considered broadly. For present purposes regulatory policy is the framework within which rules and alternatives to rules are considered, evaluated and implemented by government and public authorities seeking to influence the behaviour of private actors in the economy.

Having defined the central concepts, the scope of the present review is determined by the method adopted to collate and to ascribe importance to examples of where behavioural economics has thus far influenced public policy and, in particular, regulatory policy. The primary sources are published academic papers, policy documents and personal communications with experts and policy makers in the countries concerned. Consequently, greater emphasis is given to those examples where the influence of behavioural economics has been documented and made explicit. A policy is considered to be "behaviourally informed" if one or more findings of behavioural economics is a factor in its design or in the decision regarding whether or not to proceed with it.

2.3 "Nudge"

In the United States and the United Kingdom, the now considerable impact of behavioural economics on policy has largely come about by way of one highly influential approach, due to the work of Richard Thaler and Cass Sunstein. These authors have pioneered a principle for the application of behavioural economics to policy, which they initially termed "libertarian paternalism" (Thaler and Sunstein, 2003) and later labelled "nudge" (the title of Thaler and Sunstein's, 2008, popular book). The concept applies to circumstances where an authority has responsibility for an environment in which actors make suboptimal decisions. A nudge has two defining features: first, the authority preserves free choice by not preventing selection of apparently suboptimal options and, second, the findings of behavioural science are employed to alter the decision context in a way that makes better decisions more likely. In the jargon, the authority sets the "choice architecture" such that the sought after benefit materialises through free choice. This approach of course assumes that the authority concerned can determine that the new outcome represents a welfare improvement, i.e. that we know when decisions are "better". This assumption is not uncontroversial (Beshears et al., 2008; Sugden, 2011; see Subsection 4.4). Translating the debate into the terminology of regulatory policy tools, to justify introducing a nudge requires a positive regulatory impact analysis, in which the authority is able not only to calculate *ex-ante* outcomes following the nudge but also to show how these outcomes represent an improvement.

Whether an intervention counts as a nudge in part depends on the perspective adopted. For instance, in markets where consumers appear to be taking suboptimal decisions by selecting disadvantageous deals, a proposed nudge might involve a standardised form of product information disclosure that aims to make product comparison easier, perhaps by making the disadvantages salient. Thus, consumers can continue to select the apparently disadvantageous deals if they really want to, but are nudged towards better ones. Yet an element of compulsion is nevertheless involved in any regulation that mandates a certain type of information disclosure or prevents others. The mandate does limit the firm's choice-set and, by extension, the availability to consumers of firms that do not wish to describe their products as mandated. In other words, the distinction between a nudge and an intervention that is not a nudge is not entirely clean. In practice, nudges may to some extent constrain the choices of some economic actors, often firms. A notable example is the reform of domestic energy tariffs being introduced in the United Kingdom by OFGEM (see subsection 4.1).

Most importantly, despite frequently being identified with each other, behavioural economics and nudging are distinct concepts. One is positive, the other normative. Behavioural economics is a scientific discipline (or subdiscipline), while nudging is one potential way to apply the results of that discipline to policy making. To advocate nudging is to adopt a normative position regarding how the scientific results *should* be used. Whatever the merits of this position, it is important to note that it cannot be inferred from the scientific results themselves. Examples that illustrate this point appear at various points throughout this review.

As a scientific subdiscipline with an increasingly diverse set of findings, behavioural economics has the potential to do much more for policy makers than to assist in designing nudges. To give one concrete example, regulators who enforce competition policy can employ insights from behavioural economics to assist them in market analyses, thereby supplementing traditional approaches based on the economics of industrial organisation. Behavioural analysis can help regulators to understand such matters as the ability of an incumbent firm to maintain a monopolistic position despite apparent competition, or the reluctance of consumers in some markets to switch to seemingly lower cost suppliers. Stucke (2012) provides further examples of how behavioural economics can be useful for competition policy. The broader point here, however, is that this relatively new scientific subdiscipline is potentially of use to any policy maker who might benefit from better understanding of economic decisions, whether the policy under consideration is a nudge or otherwise.

3. The growing influence of behavioural economics on policy

This section presents a stock take on the rise of behaviourally informed policy making. At this stage, it is not possible to present an evaluation of the success or otherwise of the initiatives concerned, most of which are recent.

In both the United States and the United Kingdom, the influence of behavioural economics has been remarkably direct, in the sense that individuals prominent in behavioural economic research have been appointed to posts or advisory positions at the heart of government. The two most noted cases are the authors of *Nudge*. Cass Sunstein was the head of the Office of Information and Regulatory Affairs (OIRA) at the White House from 2009-2012. Richard Thaler has been an advisor to the Behavioural Insights Team at the UK Cabinet Office (hereafter UKBIT) since its establishment in 2010. In addition to the promotion of behaviourally informed thinking across government departments and its agencies, both of these central government bodies have been responsible for a good number of specific behaviourally informed initiatives.

3.1 United States

Through a series of Executive Orders and Memoranda to heads of departments and agencies, OIRA has sought to instil key behaviourally informed principles into US government regulation (see Sunstein, 2011, for details). Prominent among these is the use as a regulatory tool of "simplified disclosure" (see Subsection 4.1) of information in contexts where consumers or clients make purchase or other choices, often as an alternative to more traditional "command and control" regulation. In addition to simplification, OIRA has aimed to establish the distinction between summary disclosure and full disclosure (see Subsection 4.1). The primary behavioural insight behind this initiative is that individual decision making is influenced not only by what information is available, but also by how that information is presented and framed. As well as establishing the importance of simplified disclosure as a regulatory tool, OIRA has promoted the use of other behaviourally informed principles by departments and agencies in the presentation of information, including with respect to the simplicity and salience of information provided and the setting of beneficial defaults, which according to behavioural evidence are likely to aid good decision making.

One important aspect of these OIRA initiatives is the emphasis placed on the testing of old regulations and the monitoring of new ones for effectiveness. Policy explicitly attempts to adapt behavioural approaches to the management of the regulatory stock (Figure 2). It requires government agencies and departments to produce plans for the retrospective analysis of existing rules, and encourages them to employ scientifically controlled experiments, especially randomized experiments, to assess the effects of different information disclosures, both in prospective and retrospective analyses.

There has been a stream of other examples of behaviourally informed policies in the United States in recent years, some of which are explored in more detail in Box 2 and Section 4. Behavioural principles were involved in the design of: the 2009 CARD Act, which tightened the regulation of credit cards (Box 2); the Affordable Care Act, which reformed US health care; the regulation of product labelling in relation to food and energy; the regulation of product descriptions relating to pension plans and educational courses; several "MyData" initiatives (see Subsection 4.1) to supply consumers with useful personal data designed to improve their decisions; the redesign of administrative methods for determining the eligibility for state sponsored health care and for school lunches; a new method of receiving welfare payments; the promotion of behaviourally informed occupational pension schemes; and the replacement of the Food and Drug Administration's "food pyramid" for communicating nutritional balance with a simplified "food plate". A number of states and districts have employed behaviourally inspired policies to alter the environment in which food choices are made, many based on the work of Cornell's Center for Behavioral Economics in Child Nutrition Programmes.

The recent application of behavioural economics specifically to US financial regulation reflects the need for improved regulatory policy identified in the wake of the global financial crisis (OECD, 2012). The Dodd-Frank Wall Street Reform and Consumer Protection Act of 2010 established the Consumer Financial Protection Bureau (CFPB), with a mission to "make markets for consumer financial products and services work for Americans". Although recruitment to this new agency was initially slowed by political disputes, the CFPB is now fully operational. The CFPB has considerable regulatory power and is explicitly attempting to incorporate behavioural economics into its work.

Box 2. The CARD Act 2009

The Credit Card Accountability Responsibility and Disclosure (CARD) Act was signed into US law by President Obama in May 2009. The Act was in part motivated by a perceived need to strengthen consumer financial protection in the wake of the financial crisis. Some of the Act's provisions were explicitly designed to counter what were seen as unfair or misleading practices by US credit card companies. Several of these practices appeared to take advantage of phenomena that had been extensively documented in the behavioural economics literature and some of the provisions in the Act were informed by the insights available.

Specifically, bodies of evidence (of varying size and strength) suggest that individual decision making is not time consistent and that some consumers therefore overly discount large potential future costs when considering immediate purchases; that some consumers pay insufficient attention to potential costs, such as fees or changes in interest rates, terms and conditions; that consumers may be too optimistic when assessing the likelihood of incurring fees; that many consumers do not appreciate the non-linear compounding of interest; and that some consumers may "anchor" repayments to minimum payment information (or even treat it as advice).

The CARD Act sought to limit the negative impact of such behavioural phenomena in the credit card market, primarily through the banning of certain types of fees that seemed effectively to be "hidden" and via the mandating of lenders to supply consumers with more helpful and timely information. One of the main provisions was to force lenders to decline transactions that would exceed the credit limit rather than to charge a fee, unless the consumer explicitly stated that they would rather such transactions were honoured. New rules were also introduced to define more clearly when a payment could be classified as late, to extend the notice period for changes to rates, terms and conditions, to prohibit inactivity fees, and to limit the number and size of penalty fees. The Act also contained a particular nudge: lenders were mandated to include on bills an explicit calculation of the time and cost of repaying the balance through minimum monthly repayments, and a similar calculation for the cost of repaying over 36 months.

Given the above and the widespread use of credit cards, the CARD Act 2009 might be considered one of the most prominent applications of behavioural economics to policy thus far. While there is presently insufficient evidence to evaluate the impact fully, initial quantitative analyses of the US credit card market since the passing of the Act are encouraging. While it would be unwise to infer too much from a single study, Argawal et al. (2013) have recently estimated that the regulation of hidden fees has saved consumers USD 21 billion per year, based on data from more than 150 million accounts. They also find that the nudge involving explicit calculations on bills led to a significant impact on repayments, although this effect was small in comparison to the reduced payment of fees.

Perhaps the most prominent CFPB policy thus far is the "know before you owe" initiative, which aims to simplify information disclosures for mortgages, credit cards and student loans, based on behavioural evidence that the complexity of these financial products adversely affects consumer decision making. The CFPB has pretested prototype simplified disclosure forms with consumers. It is proposed that the new forms will be mandatory in closing documents, i.e. at the point of sale.

Another policy in the United States that is worthy of specific mention is the attempt by several cities to follow the lead of New York City in trying to ban the sale of sugary carbonated drinks above a certain size – a policy intended to counter obesity, especially among children. Evidence derived from behavioural research is a partial motivation for the proposed ban, but behavioural evidence has been prominent on both sides of the vociferous debate about the merits and demerits of this regulation. Behavioural research relating to social norms, self-control, the power of defaults and the perception of portion size has been used to support the ban, while research relating to substitution, potential alternatives and responses to coercion has been cited in opposition to it. Although announced in May 2012, at the time of writing the ban in New York City remains blocked by legal challenge.

It is worth noting that the proposed carbonated drinks ban is an example where policy makers have employed behavioural research in relation to a proposed regulatory policy that is antithetical to the nudge philosophy. Indeed, the fight against obesity is one policy challenge where some independent scientists argue that the available research suggests more strident interventions than nudges may be required if policy is to have genuine impact (see House of Lords Science and Technology Committee, 2011). It is clearly possible that the available behavioural research could support such a proposition, in line with the distinction between positive and normative analysis made above. As regards obesity this remains highly controversial, both in the scientific and policy making communities.

Lastly, in summer 2013 the US federal government began hiring researchers to staff its own version of UKBIT. The stated aim of the new initiative is:

> *... to scale behavioural interventions that have been rigorously evaluated, using, where possible, randomized controlled trials.*
> (US government, 2013)

3.2 United Kingdom

Although established centrally in the UK's Cabinet Office in 2010, UKBIT was not set up as top-down issuer of executive orders or guidelines, but to work more like an internal public sector consultancy. Its work therefore presents something of a contrast to the influence of behavioural economics on US policy making. UKBIT's interventions have been developed collaboratively with government departments, agencies and the private sector, including the orchestration of policy trials at a local level. Two detailed examples are provided in Box 3. UKBIT is now assisting the Australian government to establish some similar initiatives. In May 2013, however, the Cabinet Office announced that UKBIT would be "spun out", meaning that it is to become a profit-making venture with a commercial partner. At the time of writing it is unclear whether and how this development will alter its work. The stated intention is for UKBIT to continue to service the UK government through the Cabinet Office, and to meet any international demand from public and private entities with a "public good ethos".

Box 3. Two examples of interventions designed by the UK Behavioural Insights Team

Fine collection

Non-payment of fines imposed by UK courts results in considerable state expenditure as the authorities seek to secure payment. UKBIT has worked alongside Her Majesty's Courts and Tribunal Service (HMCTS) to use behavioural insights in order improve repayment rates.

The findings of behavioural economics suggest that small but immediate costs, in terms of time, effort and money, can have disproportionate effects on whether people will undertake actions that are beneficial in the long run (see Subsection 4.2). This evidence suggests that a proportion of those who owe fines will not bring themselves to make the payment, even though it makes sense to pay a fine promptly in order to avoid being charged for late or non-payment, or for the fee of the bailiffs sent to recover the debt. Employing this insight, HMCTS initially increased the rate of fine collection simply by making it more convenient for people to pay by numerous methods, and by issuing reminders by text and telephone.

Other behavioural findings suggest that personalising communications can increase the likelihood that individuals act on them (Garner, 2005). To test whether this effect might translate into better policy, UKBIT devised a Randomised Controlled Trial (RCT) to assess the effectiveness of personalised communications to fine defaulters. The initial results suggest that the personalised message is more effective (Behavioural Insights Team, 2012a).

This is therefore an example where behavioural economics can be used to improve the effectiveness of a policy without the need for new or tougher regulations.

Box 3. **Two examples of interventions designed by the UK Behavioural Insights Team** (*cont.*)

Loft clearance schemes

Large numbers of UK households would benefit in the long run from improving their home insulation, which would also reduce carbon emissions. UKBIT has organised a series of trials that use behavioural science to devise a range of methods to encourage households to install better insulation.

The primary problem to overcome, according to behavioural economic research, is that householders are likely to weigh immediate costs disproportionately relative to benefits that only accrue over many years. Further evidence suggests that while householders can be sure of the size of the immediate costs, they may be more uncertain about the scale of future benefits, increasing the extent to which they discount them when considering whether to improve insulation. One further potentially relevant insight is that when they are unsure about decisions people often copy the decisions of others around them.

UKBIT's trials, conducted in partnership with local authorities and retailers, used this evidence to design and to test four behavioural mechanisms for their potential to increase the take-up of insulation: an upfront reward (a voucher, a one-month holiday from local taxation); discounts for signing up neighbours for energy efficiency improvements; subsidised loft clearance; and community rewards for signing up additional households for energy efficiency improvements.

Given the existing evidence, it is very difficult to predict which of these schemes is most likely to produce the strongest impact on householders' decision making. While full comparative results are not yet published, one perhaps surprising finding to emerge from the trials is that the impact of subsidising loft clearance turned out to be particularly strong, resulting in a four-fold increase in the odds of installing loft insulation. This is a telling example of the inductive scientific approach being incorporated into the development of policy itself, such that hypotheses are tested directly in the policy domain.

UKBIT's work on health policy mostly surrounds public health. The initiatives include: changing the default choice for organ donation; negotiating a voluntary agreement for a gradual (and hence, for consumers, a largely unnoticed) reduction in the salt content of pre-prepared food; and the trialling of some strategies to reduce smoking and alcohol consumption. UKBIT has also trialled some behaviourally informed interventions aimed at improving the performance of the UK's National Health Service, such as changing the design of hospital prescription charts to improve accuracy and experimenting with different forms of communication with patients to reduce the number of missed appointments.

UKBIT has also contributed to the United Kingdom's new consumer policy strategy (Department of Business, Innovation and Skills, 2011), which incorporates a number of behavioural insights into policies presently at varying stages of implementation. Most of the new policies draw on one of two areas of behavioural research: the framing of information and behavioural convergence.

With respect to framing, behavioural findings have repeatedly shown that actors make different decisions when presented with information framed in different ways. In particular, simplifying information can alter both decisions and decision makers' willingness to engage with a particular decision (Iyengar and Kamenica, 2010). The proposed UK consumer policies aim to simplify and standardise the provision of information to consumers in certain markets. The initial regulatory policy areas in question are: credit cards, energy tariffs, energy performance certificates, food hygiene ratings and car labels. Research is also being funded to identify more effective ways to communicate product information in relation to health and the environment. As in the United States, the United Kingdom is also trying to introduce a "MyData" initiative. These types of policies entail costs, both in the need to fund initial research to identify forms of information disclosure that assist consumer decision making, and in the requirement for businesses to comply with the regulations and/or voluntary agreements that impose the information disclosure standard. The logic is that these costs will be small relative to returns in terms of better consumer decision making.

"Behavioural convergence" is an umbrella term for the now well-established tendency for decision makers to be swayed by the decisions of others (Rafaat et al., 2009). Similar phenomena include herding, information cascades and bandwagon effects. UK consumer policy is looking to turn this tendency to consumers' advantage through the regulation of customer feedback and online comparison websites, the provision of similar "choice-tools" for public services, and the disclosure of complaint data.

Another prominent area of activity for UKBIT is tax compliance. The unit has made use of a series of randomised controlled trials (RCTs) to explore the impact of different forms of behaviourally informed communication to those who are not paying taxes, in collaboration with the tax authorities. Some of these RCTs have produced clear, statistically significant effects associated with different types of communication, which if widely rolled out may save considerable sums in recovered tax and reduced enforcement costs. UKBIT have applied a similar approach also to fine defaulters (Box 3).

Other areas in which UKBIT has trialled interventions include energy conservation, where trials of multiple interventions have thrown up some surprising results (Box 3). This underlines the benefits of adopting an empirical approach to policy design. The unit has also trialled interventions in the areas of employment activation and charitable giving. More broadly, it aims to spread the use of empirical approaches to policy design (see Behavioural Insights Team, 2011, 2012a, 2012b, for detail).

Prior to the establishment of UKBIT, behavioural economics was already featuring strongly in the work of the UK's Office of Fair Trading (OFT), which is responsible for the enforcement of consumer and competition law. The agency has been prominent in commissioning and conducting its own behavioural research projects, including original experimental work designed to address specific questions of interest for policy (see Section 5). As with the establishment of the CFPB in the United States, in 2013 the United Kingdom also created a new regulatory agency for financial services, the Financial Conduct Authority (FCA). The FCA has recruited behavioural economists and made it an explicit aim to employ behavioural economics in its work. A recent report authored by FCA staff (Erta et al., 2013) concludes that behavioural economics has potential implications for the way the FCA creates policy rules and guidance, analyses firm behaviour, builds evidence for enforcement cases and regulates communications with consumers.

3.3 The European Commission

The European Commission has engaged with behavioural economics, initially through the work of DG SANCO (the commission's health and consumer directorate) and latterly through the work of the Joint Research Centre (JRC), which is in the process of establishing a Behavioural Economics Taskforce. Van Bavel et al. (2013) provide a recent account of the growing influence of behavioural economics in European Union policy making, together with a guide to conducting behavioural studies within policy domains.

The Consumer Rights Directive, which was proposed in 2008 and, at the time of writing, is being transposed into the domestic law of European Union (EU) member states, contains two consumer protection provisions that are directly informed by behavioural research. The first limits the use of pre-ticked boxes in consumer contracts, based on behavioural findings that reveal the strong impact that default settings can have on consumer decisions (see Box 1). The second introduces a cooling-off period after the initial agreement of consumer contracts, during which consumers have the right to change their mind. This regulation is informed by behavioural research on inconsistent preferences, the influence of mood on decision making and consumer responses to sales techniques.

Regulation to support the European Single Market is a key function of the Commission and it has recently increased its use of behavioural studies that address specific research questions for regulatory design. The first of these involved the funding of a series of experiments to explore how consumers choose between retail investment products and how they are affected by financial advice (European Commission, 2010). The aim of this project was to inform the design of better financial regulation and the research questions addressed were selected specifically for their potential contribution to this aim. Since this first study, the Commission has undertaken a range of similarly targeted behavioural research projects relating to consumer issues in different markets, including: consumer rights relating to travel packages, tobacco labelling and packaging, CO_2 labelling for cars, food information, energy labelling, online gambling, transparency of bank charges, European sales law and fees for international credit card use. The JRC is now expanding the use of behavioural studies, including with respect to EU public health policy in the areas of obesity, physical activity and cancer screening. In these cases, the application of behavioural economics to policy is at an early stage, where behavioural evidence is being gathered that is specific to the policy context, but it seems likely that concrete applications will follow.

In addition to the examples cited above, the European Commission has employed behavioural economics in the context of the prominent competition case taken against Microsoft. The chosen remedy in this case, which relates to the bundling of Microsoft's operating system and web browser, is to ensure that consumers who purchase the operating system face an active decision regarding which browser they wish to use, rather than gravitating towards a default browser.

3.4 Other countries

While the United States and United Kingdom have arguably pioneered the application of behavioural economics to policy, there are many significant and innovative applications in other countries. Certain behaviourally informed policies have now spread internationally. In some countries institutions have adopted or even been established specifically to champion behavioural thinking. Several governments have made efforts to spread knowledge of relevant behavioural findings among policy makers, perhaps most notably among economic regulators. This section summarises these developments.

One policy area in which behavioural economics has been applied in a number of countries is pension policy, partly because the empirical evidence in this area is straightforward and demonstrable. Despite the existence of strong financial incentives, many workers save insufficiently for retirement, often by their own admission, and their decisions can be dramatically altered by how the particular pension scheme frames the choices available. Pension coverage and contribution rates are influenced by whether the default requires them to opt in or opt out of the scheme and whether workers are given the opportunity to pre-commit to increasing contributions at a later stage (e.g. Madrian and Shea, 2001; Thaler and Benartzi, 2004). These and subsequent findings have informed pension reform in a number of countries, including the United States, New Zealand, Australia, Italy and the United Kingdom.

The pattern whereby specific behavioural findings have a relatively rapid impact on a particular policy area across a number of countries does not apply to only pension policy. Another example is retail display bans for sales of cigarettes, which are informed by empirical evidence on impulse purchases, the role of salience in decision making and the behavioural impact of exposure to cigarette marketing (e.g. Department of Health, 2008). Bans have now been introduced in Australia, Canada, Finland, Iceland, Ireland, New Zealand, Norway and the United Kingdom. The aforementioned work on how the nature of communications from the authorities can increase tax compliance (e.g. Behavioural Insights Team, 2012a) has also spread internationally. Such experimental approaches to tax compliance, including in many cases the use of RCTs, have now been undertaken in the United States, the United Kingdom, Sweden, Australia and Israel.

In a number of countries, a key institution or organisation has led or is leading a process aimed at capturing the attention of policy makers and alerting them to the potential of behavioural economics for improving policy. Notable cases described briefly here are Australia, France, Denmark, and Norway.

In Australia, the Productivity Commission, which is a state research and advisory body, has held a series of events and produced a number of reports aimed at applying behavioural thinking to public policy generally (Productivity Commission, 2008a) and to certain specific policy areas, including an examination of the implications for consumer policy (Productivity Commission, 2008b) and a broad applied behavioural analysis of gambling behaviour and policy (Productivity Commission, 2010). The Department of Finance and Deregulation (2012) also recently published its own account of the insights offered by behavioural economics for regulatory policy, concluding that while applications of behavioural economics are not yet widespread "its advancement is encouraged to be explored further" (p. 56).

A similar role has been undertaken for the French government by the Centre d'analyse stratégique, which (until a recent reorganisation) was a research body under the direct supervision of the office of the Prime Minister. The Centre concentrated its research efforts on the implications of behavioural science for environmental and public health policy. Its reports developed policy options for employing behavioural science to reduce smoking and obesity (Centre d'analyse stratégique, 2010) and for promoting more environmentally responsible behaviour such as recycling, energy saving and litter prevention (Centre d'analyse stratégique, 2011).

In contrast to a model where behaviourally informed policy design is promoted by a government unit, agency or research institute, both Denmark and Norway have active organisations outside of government that are promoting applications of behavioural economics in a more bottom-up fashion. In Denmark, "iNudgeYou" is a not-for-profit organisation dedicated to improving decisions. It has established a network of public and private sector partners and engages in small scale experimentation, micro-interventions and training, designed to spread knowledge about effective interventions to achieve desirable behaviour change without limiting choice. In other words, it promotes one particular use of behavioural economics – nudging – as a solution to a range of public policy problems. In Norway, GreeNudge has a similar philosophy and also operates in a bottom-up manner, though its work concentrates on policies that affect climate change, such as policies and private sector initiatives to cut waste and increase energy efficiency (e.g. Kalbekken et al., 2013).

Most of the above examples document applications of behavioural economics to policy that have been driven by overarching policy instruments (e.g. OIRA Executive Orders in the United States), or by the establishment of specialised policy units, agencies or non-governmental organisations. In each case, the promotion of behaviourally informed thinking is identified with a particular institution or group of individuals. These *explicit* mechanisms for applying behavioural economics to policy might be contrasted with more *implicit* ones, whereby understanding of behavioural economics is spread more broadly among policy makers across a sweep of institutions within the public sector. Instead of a group of individuals with specialist knowledge seeking to apply behavioural ideas across policy areas, it may be possible for policy makers within these areas to absorb and apply behavioural thinking.

In the past five years, many governments have hosted conferences and training workshops, or commissioned and disseminated research reports with the intention of informing public officials of the main findings of behavioural economics and encouraging them to consider how its insights might apply to their policy area. Such initiatives have taken place in at least the following countries: Australia, Denmark, France, Ireland, New Zealand, Norway, Sweden, the United Kingdom and the United States. The European Commission has also hosted international events on applying behavioural economics to policy. Some of these initiatives have examined the potential use of behavioural economics across the entire sweep of public policy, while others have focused on regulatory policy, in many cases consumer and competition policy.

As highlighted in Section 1, there is a danger of underestimating the importance of the more implicit influence of behavioural economics and the extent to which behavioural thinking is spreading among regulatory policy makers in particular. Developments in the Nordic nations are particularly interesting in this regard. While explicit applications of behavioural economics to policy are presently less prominent in these countries than in the United States or the United Kingdom, policy makers and researchers in Denmark and Sweden in particular articulate the view that behavioural economics is becoming rapidly influential because its implications are consistent with traditional modes of governance. Specifically, Nordic governments have a history of more paternalistic policy making, in the sense that there is greater willingness for government to be involved in individual economic decision making than in most other developed nations. The populations in the Nordic countries also have a measurably high degree of trust in government by international standards.

There are some prominent historical examples in Sweden where intuitive behavioural thinking underpinned previous policy initiatives. These include the design of a decades-old scheme designed to help young workers save, which employed automatic contributions from employers, restrictions on withdrawals and incentives in the form of lotteries – all three of which could have been designed by a behavioural economist based on modern scientific findings on defaults, time discounting and the overestimation of small probabilities. Similarly, in an effort to increase the attention Swedes give to their retirement savings, since 1999 the government has sent all taxpayers a bright orange envelope containing a pension statement complete with personalised projections (cf. Subsection 4.3 on salience).

There are indications that the adoption of behavioural ideas is proceeding among policy makers in the Nordic nations, particularly in the area of economic regulation. In Denmark, the Danish Competition and Consumer Agency, the Danish Business Association and the Danish Tax

Authorities have all begun to engage with behavioural economics and to use it in their work. For instance, the Danish Competition and Consumer Authority has recently employed behavioural scientists and organised quite extensive training in behavioural economics for its staff. It is presently proposing, among other initiatives, a behaviourally informed approach to encouraging switching among bank customers and to the regulation of financial advice. In Sweden, the Swedish Consumer Agency has revised its method of consumer market analysis to encompass behavioural insights. It is presently proposing new behaviourally informed price regulations for mobile telephones and the initiation of empirical studies on real-time feedback mechanisms in the mobile and broadband market. In the Netherlands, the Authority for Consumers & Markets has recently conducted a project on the implications of behavioural economics for its work, increasing its emphasis on the demand side of the markets it regulates.

3.5 Which policy types and policy areas?

Taken as a whole, this overview of the many places and policy areas where behavioural economics is proving influential is sufficient to reveal a strong relationship between behavioural economics and regulatory policy. Taking Lowi's (1972) classic four-way policy typology (distributive, constituent, redistributive and regulatory policies), where the examples above do not relate to a regulatory policy, they often relate to the search for alternative and perhaps less coercive ways to achieve the same result. For instance, altering the nature of communications with taxpayers as a way of achieving tax compliance or changing the default option for pension enrolment, are attempts to avoid the expense and other negative consequences of stronger coercion – a constituent policy is sought to do the job of an otherwise tougher regulation. That said, there are some examples of behaviourally informed policies above that sit squarely in the categories of distributive and redistributive policy, such as where behavioural economics is used to improve the quality of service delivery, or to assist the poor to access financial services. Nevertheless, the preponderance of examples referred to in this section, which total more than 60 separate instances where behavioural economics has influenced policy, either relate to regulatory policy or to a search for alternatives to regulation.

Furthermore, within regulatory policy, behavioural economics appears to have made particularly strong inroads with respect to consumer policy. This partly reflects the simple fact that very many of the decisions people make when interacting with non-family members or organisations are made as consumers. Improved understanding of decision making is likely, therefore, to improve understanding of consumer choices and thus of the factors driving desirable or undesirable outcomes.

Moreover, policy makers in the areas of competition and consumer protection are increasingly finding common cause, since the evidence unearthed by behavioural economics is resulting in greater recognition of the possibility that disadvantageous consumer choices are not only harmful to the specific decision maker, but potentially undermine the effectiveness of competition in ensuring downward pressure on prices and upward pressure on quality. Competition policy makers, who have traditionally concentrated on market structure and its interaction with firm behaviour, are therefore paying greater attention to the demand side of the market and how firms might seek to exploit systematic consumer behaviours that may not, ultimately, be in consumers' best interests. This is consequently a clear example where the findings of behavioural economics are weakening the grip on policy of the traditional neo-classical microeconomic model.

That behavioural economics has made its greatest inroads in consumer policy does not necessarily imply that its implications for other areas of regulatory policy will turn out to be less important. Regulations set the context for decisions in relation to, among other things, health and safety, labour markets and environmental protection. As of now, the findings of behavioural economics appear to have had more limited impacts in these areas, although researchers have drawn attention to their potential and some policy makers have actively sought to engage with research (e.g. on health and safety, see Sapsford, Phythian-Adams and Apps, 2009; on environmental protection, see Shogren, 2012).

4. Behavioural economics and policy design

This section considers a selection of examples and case studies in more detail to draw a series of inferences about how behavioural economics is influencing regulatory policy design. It is notable that a particular subset of behavioural phenomena features strongly in the early applications of behavioural economics, namely those associated with the impact on decisions of simplicity, convenience and salience. The section then briefly considers behavioural findings that appear to have relevance to regulation but do not, as of now, feature so strongly in policy development. Lastly, it is argued that behavioural economics is having a broader influence on policy design. In addition to policies that are designed to counteract or make use of specific behavioural phenomena in order to work towards a particular policy goal, behavioural economics is influencing the method of policy design. The inductive logic that underpins behavioural work invites a similarly inductive approach to policy, leading to greater use of context specific research, experimentation, piloting and RCTs.

4.1 Simplification of information and choice

A significant proportion of the behaviourally informed policies introduced to date centres on the potential benefits of simplification. The aim is to design regulations either to simplify the presentation of information or otherwise to limit the number or complexity of options within the available choice-set, based on the assumption that such simplification will promote better decision making. This aim echoes the broader one of trying to ensure that regulations themselves are also comprehensible and clear (OECD, 2012, Recommendation 2; see also Section 5). Many examples are in the domain of consumer policy. Through regulation, firms can be mandated to provide simplified product descriptions or simplified product ranges (or in some cases both), with the intention of making it easier for consumers to assess the suitability of products or to compare products within the same market. Because of the prevalence of such regulations, both already in force and proposed, a fairly detailed treatment is offered here.

In the United States, OIRA has sought to make regulatory authorities distinguish between "summary disclosure" and "full disclosure". The former is a mandated disclosure offered at the point of sale that attempts to simplify and standardise information. The aim is to ensure that consumers know the key attributes of the product they are considering and are able more easily to compare across products within the same market. Such summary disclosure is often supplemented by regulations that require full disclosure of information online, so that consumers can look up all relevant aspects of a product or contract should they wish to. Examples of this kind of regulation include the information duties imposed following the passing of the Affordable Care Act in the United States; the CFPB's proposed mandated disclosures in relation to mortgages, credit cards and student loans; and various initiatives employing standardised product labelling, especially in the areas of food and environmental information.

A more strident attempt by UK policy makers to introduce regulations that simplify consumer choice has been made by the UK Energy Regulator, OFGEM. Evidence suggests that following the deregulation of UK energy markets, the complexity of the choices available in the market led to fewer active consumers than expected and to some consumers making poor choices (OFGEM, 2011, 2012). Indeed, Giulietti, Waddams Price and Waterson (2005) and Wilson and Waddams Price (2010) have shown that many consumers remain on more expensive tariffs, mostly with incumbent suppliers, while most of those who do switch suppliers fail to locate the best deal, with a substantial minority even switching to a less beneficial contract. OFGEM initially proposed strong regulation to simplify the choice between tariffs: the regulator was to set the standing charge and energy suppliers would compete only over the unit rate charge. Following consultation and the expression of concerns about serving niche markets (e.g. low energy users who might want a low standing charge), later proposals have abandoned fixing the standing charge by regulation, but still aim to introduce relatively strong regulations to simplify tariffs, including banning tariffs with more than two tiers, limiting the number of tariffs each company can offer, and mandating disclosure of the cheapest tariff together with calculations of the related savings. In other words, OFGEM are seeking both to mandate how suppliers provide information about each offering and to limit the complexity of the range of tariffs each supplier offers.

The assumption that simplification of the information and choices facing decision makers will improve decisions is partly backed by empirical evidence on the phenomenon of "choice overload". Beginning with Iyengar and Lepper (2000), evidence has accumulated to suggest that when decision makers are faced with multiple or complex choices it can have a negative effect on their decisions. This can happen because decision makers appear to react to the perceived complexity of the information itself. Two types of negative outcome have been documented: failure to select the best options when more than a few options are available, and unwillingness to make an active choice at all when faced with a more complex decision. In addition to experiments involving choices between everyday consumer goods, examples of these phenomena have been recorded with financial products such as pension plans and loans (e.g. Iyengar, Huberman & Jiang, 2004; Agnew and Szykman, 2005; Iyengar and Kamenica, 2010; Bertrand et al., 2010).

The reform of the Swedish pension system is an oft-cited example of where policy makers failed to consider the effects of choice overload. In this case, the very large range available pension plans, which ran to several hundred, may well have contributed to the majority of workers opting for default plans rather than engaging with the very complex array of products and making an active choice.

The logic of employing regulation to simplify the choices facing consumers, perhaps most forcefully articulated by Sunstein (2011), has intuitive appeal, especially in relation to products such as financial services, insurance and consumer service contracts. Simplified disclosure is also likely to be popular with consumers. Over and above its potential for improved decision making, simplified and standardised product descriptions may help to improve market efficiency through reduced transaction and switching costs, particularly in terms of time and effort.

Yet while the mandating of simplified information has some scientific backing, is intuitively appealing and may prove popular, there are some reasons to be cautious in the application of regulations designed to simplify product descriptions or product ranges. It is worth noting that the science of choice overload is not uncontroversial. Some early choice overload experiments have failed to replicate and it is not fully understood why some studies show large effects of complexity on willingness to take decisions, or satisfaction with decisions, while other studies do not (Scheibehenne, Greifeneder and Todd, 2010). Furthermore, although consumers are likely to welcome simplification, they may be unaware of any contribution to costs and hence potentially to prices of compliance with the mandate. Since there are likely to be such costs, the scale of the benefits is important to assess empirically.

There are some examples of mandated summary disclosures where evidence of effectiveness is not encouraging. These include regulations on simplified mortgage disclosure in the United Kingdom, which were introduced in 2004. The Mortgage Conduct of Business (MCOB) aimed to provide consumers with intelligible information in a highly prescribed format to assist comparison of offerings. Evidence suggests that MCOB increased business costs, leading to higher prices, with no discernible decrease in price dispersion (Monteiro and Zaidi, 2007), as might have been anticipated had consumers made better choices. Similarly, the helpfulness of the US Securities and Exchange Commission's "Summary Prospectus" for mutual funds has been questioned by a controlled experiment which found that the summary did not prevent investors from selecting funds with higher fees (Beshears et al., 2010). On the other hand, a recent study of the effects of a mandated product standardisation in Massachusetts, US, finds that it has had a measurable impact on consumer choice and led to better consumer outcomes (Marzilli Ericson and Starc, 2013).

Much more empirical work is needed to understand when and how the simplification of information improves decisions. Given the contrasting findings above, it is important that new disclosure regulations are evaluated for effectiveness. In most cases, there is no reason not to pre-test the specific form of simplified disclosure proposed for its effectiveness on decision making, either through a laboratory experiment, field experiment or trial. This logic underpins a number of ongoing EU studies and the work of the CFPB, among others.

One possibility, implied by the previous studies, is that choices in such complex markets as those for retail financial services may need not only to be simpler, but to be very much simpler, before reliable effects on consumer behaviour can be measured. Experimental research undertaken by the European Commission (2010) shows beneficial effects on consumer choice of simplifying information relating to retail investment products, but the choice in the experiment was arguably unrealistically simple in comparison with any choices faced by consumers in real markets.

Thaler and Sunstein (2008) proposed an alternative method to reduce the complexity of consumer choices in markets where suppliers can gather over time consumption and transaction data specific to individual consumers. The idea is to mandate firms to provide the historical data, on request, in standardised electronic form. For example, telecommunications companies can be mandated to make available standardised data on the consumer's usage over the preceding period. This could then be uploaded and analysed by software designed to undertake price comparisons or search for deals that offer a good match for the specific consumer's usage pattern. In effect, such a system of disclosure might allow consumers to check how their present contract compares with others, to locate the best deal, or at least to reduce the choice-set down to a manageable size.

Some initiatives based on this idea have begun recently and have been labelled "MyData" (or "MiData" in the United Kingdom). The US Department of Energy and the UK Department of Business Innovation and Skills have been seeking agreement with the relevant business sectors to introduce MyData schemes on a voluntary basis. In the latter case, however, the UK government legislated in 2013 to provide the power to introduce regulations that will compel companies to supply the data on request. The focus in the United Kingdom is on four markets: energy, mobile phones, current accounts and credit cards. A similar consumer right to standardised personal consumption and transaction data is also contained in the current draft of new EU Data Protection Regulations.

MyData initiatives presently concentrate on markets in which consumers sign contracts for the ongoing supply of services. The premise is that some markets offer far too great a range of available contracts for even the most sophisticated consumer with sufficient time on their hands to locate the best deals for their requirements. Automated product and price comparisons hence constitute a form of simplification of the consumer's choice, allowing consumers at least to narrow down their options or rule out plainly disadvantageous deals. At this stage, the benefits of such a policy and the scale of the potential costs imposed on businesses in the sectors concerned are unknown. Furthermore, it is likely that the MyData initiative will have a more beneficial effect for some types of consumers than others. While the aim is to simplify consumer choice, a base level of competency in understanding the potential use of data and being able to handle computer files is required on the part of the consumer.

Overall, from the perspective of evidence informed policy, there appears to be a general trend regarding regulations designed to simplify choices. In many markets, there is evidence that complexity of choice can have detrimental effects on decisions. Yet there is often less evidence to indicate the likely success or otherwise of regulatory interventions designed to simplify the specific choices at issue. Thus, in many cases, simplification appears to be a good principle based on the generalisation of results across choice domains, but particular attempts to simplify often lack supporting evidence. Behavioural economics is therefore pointing the finger at complexity of choice and assisting regulators to identify instances of consumer detriment, but there is a need for more empirical investigation and evaluation of the outcomes of specific interventions if the costs of regulation are to be justified.

4.2 Defaults and convenience

The above examples of simplification primarily relate to the complexity of the choice set: how many options are there and how easy is it to compare between them. Evidence from behavioural economics suggests that the decision process matters too.

The most straightforward manifestation of this is the power of defaults. Decision makers are disproportionately drawn towards default options, such that changing the default can change a large proportion of decisions. Consequently, where regulatory policy has the power to determine the default option, it also has considerable potential power to determine decisions.

As described above, these findings have already had an international impact on the rules surrounding pension policy, such that some governments either incentivise or compel pension schemes to be provided on an opt-out rather than opt-in basis. Auto-enrolment into pension schemes has become a classic nudge – a change in the choice architecture of a major financial decision that alters decisions in a desired direction without denying other options. Perhaps the most useful case study thus far is the introduction of "KiwiSaver" in New Zealand, the primary feature of which is auto-enrolment. In the four years following its introduction in 2007, pension coverage increased by almost 50 percentage points. Not all of this increase can be accounted for purely by the changed default setting, as some additional subsidies were also introduced along with the new scheme. Nevertheless, the increase is initially impressive. Yet there is some evidence that KiwiSaver has reduced the amount of saving via other means, and auto-enrolment schemes can have other relevant side-effects. Most notably, a significant proportion of those who are defaulted into the scheme select the default plan and contribution rate, which may be set at a relatively low level. For a more detailed account see OECD (2013a).

It remains the case that the majority of developed nations have a compulsory second-tier pension. Despite the power of defaults and the apparent success of auto-enrolment in raising coverage, the behavioural evidence on time discounting may be the greater issue for this policy area. Individuals tend to prioritise spending in the present over spending in the future and many suffer reductions in spending power at retirement as a result. It is unclear whether a nudge is sufficient to change this pattern, should policy makers decide that it is appropriate to do so. Higher compulsory saving may be the more viable option (OECD, 2013a).

Behavioural economics may nevertheless feature prominently in a compulsory saving scheme, as with the recently reformed Australian pension system. The reforms were, in the words of their architect, "...an adaptation of contemporary thinking in the field of behavioural economics." (Cooper et al., 2010, p. 9). Superannuation contributions are compulsory in Australia above a low income limit, but the new regulations establish a default fund called "MySuper" for workers who do not engage and thus do not make active decisions regarding how their fund is invested. MySuper funds are offered by multiple providers but are strongly regulated, the aim being to ensure a safe investment standard and to prevent the charging of excessive fees. Most Australians stick with the default fund, but those who wish to take more active decisions regarding their pension funds are free to do so.

Another area where research on the power of defaults has contributed to the design of policy relates to organ donation. In 2011 the United Kingdom changed the regulations surrounding the granting of driving licences such that those applying for a licence are now compelled to make an active choice about whether or not to be an organ donor. That is, there is no default choice, applicants must tick one box or the other on the form when applying. The behavioural evidence that informed this policy shows donation rates to be dramatically higher where being an organ donor is decided by opting out rather than opting in (Johnson and Goldstein, 2003).

In the United States, OIRA has directed all federal agencies to consider the issue of how to set regulatory defaults to achieve policy goals, yet an important issue in the policy design is the difficulty of deciding on the appropriate default. In the cases of pensions and organ donation, there is widespread agreement that there is a need to increase provision and donation rates respectively. Furthermore, where people are forced to make an active choice, decisions more closely match opt-out rates than opt-in rates (Carroll et al., 2009). In other policy areas defaults may be more controversial, such as in relation to methods of making or receiving payments to and from government, choice of school, or responsibilities following the breakdown of relationships. Forcing an active choice may not be appropriate where decision makers lack the resources or capability to make a good choice – they might welcome the comfort of a default option. In general, however, deciding on the appropriate default requires a balance that takes into account whether decision makers are able to make informed choices, the actual decisions of those who make informed choices, and the degree of heterogeneity in informed decisions. Setting a good default is harder where individuals are likely to differ strongly in preferences. In some circumstances, it may be possible to set different defaults for different people, based on personal characteristics.

Designing a good policy is made more awkward by the fact that the reasons why defaults are so powerful are not fully understood. A combination of factors may well be involved. Default options may be chosen because they are perceived to be endorsed by whatever authority determines the default, i.e. that they are treated as a form of advice. Or defaults may act as a signal as to the choices made by others, leading people to be drawn towards them through behavioural convergence. In other cases, the default may not so much draw people towards it as stick them to it. Sticky defaults can emerge simply from procrastination or inertia – people failing to get around to making a decision and/or acting on it. Lastly, defaults might serve as a psychological reference point, against which other options are judged. Since each of these four possible explanations has a different implication for the likely quality of the decision, understanding which is driving behaviour might be important for policy design. This observation means that policy may need to be informed by research that is specific to the context in which choices are being made.

As well as defaults set by government, regulators might need to take an interest in defaults set by firms, who can exploit the power of defaults to influence customers' choices or to default them into more purchases, e.g. where following an introductory offer a contract begins unless the customer actively opts out of it. The defaulting of customers into products when making online purchases has resulted already in new regulations in the EU Consumer Rights Directive (Box 1).

Closely related to the power of defaults are convenience effects. The convenience of the process associated with selecting an option can have a disproportionate effect on the likelihood that it is selected, i.e. individuals seem to be drawn towards options that are easier to execute. This is an important generalisation to emerge from a range of attempts to inform policy design through behavioural science. Options that are made easy and offered at a timely moment are substantially more attractive to decision makers. A field experiment conducted by Tufano (2011) provides a nice example. When recipients of a tax refund were presented with an easy to execute option to buy a specific savings bond at the time of the refund, a much larger proportion opted to save part of their refund. Such convenience effects may be driven by more than the lowering of immediate transaction costs, since the implication of an authority or other organisation making an option convenient is that it is a popular choice, or perhaps an advisable one.

The regularity with which such "convenience effects" are observed implies that convenience is a reliable indicator of likely behaviour and needs to be considered in good policy design. Thus, where a regulation aims to induce a particular behaviour, such as compliance, it is likely to be more effective if it makes the desirable option as convenient as possible.

Small frictions can have large impacts. An example from the United States is provided by Bettinger et al. (2009), who used a randomised experiment to show that young people from low- to moderate-income families who received assistance with completing the necessary enrolment forms had an increased likelihood of going to college. This study constituted supporting evidence for changes to the Free Application for Federal Student Aid (FAFSA) form, designed to make it easier to fill out.

It might initially appear strange that such small-scale inconveniences can affect decisions that have the potential to determine long-term prospects. The relative costs and benefits of long-term outcomes seem disproportionately greater than the apparently small costs associated with the short-term processes. Again, policy might be assisted by a better understanding of the precise reasons for this influence of convenience in decisions. As with default options, individuals may treat convenient options as signals that indicate recommended or popular options. An alternative way to conceive of the issue is to consider why it is that less convenient options are disproportionately off-putting. Often, the short term cost of inconvenience is immediate and of certain magnitude, whereas the benefit that is supposedly to follow will only materialise well into the future and is of less certain magnitude. Large volumes of research find that people often discount the future steeply and respond more to losses than equivalent gains (for reviews see, respectively, Frederick, Loewenstein and O'Donohue, 2002; Rick, 2012).

4.3 Salience and attention

Decision makers can pay attention to a limited number of attributes associated with any given option in front of them. There is evidence that more salient characteristics of decisions or options can hold sway over characteristics that may be as important but are not as salient. Arguably, many regulations were designed with an intuitive understanding of the importance of salience long before behavioural economics studied salience effects more formally. Simple examples of regulatory attempts to increase salience include consumer warnings, which might be mandated on packaging or within disclosures, or the highlighting of punishments for non-compliance.

The potential power of salience to influence choices is underscored by behavioural studies in which the outcomes of transactions (money spent and items available) are held constant while the salience of different components of the price is manipulated. Examples include Hossain and Morgan (2006), who found that buyers' willingness to pay in an online auction was affected by the proportion of the price designated as a shipping cost, and Chetty, Looney and Kroft (2009), who showed that alcohol purchases were reduced more by a tax made salient on the price tag than by an equivalent tax levied at the till. Disadvantageous decisions can arise from either weighting a particularly salient feature too strongly or not giving sufficient weight to an important non-salient feature – often called "inattention".

These findings are important for regulatory policy design because they highlight a clear limitation of the orthodox economic approach to price elasticities. The results imply that elasticities may be strongly affected by the salience of a price change and/or its individual components. Where policy makers are looking to bring about a specific change in behaviour, perhaps a reduction or increase in the consumption of a product with long-term health consequences, the salience of the tax is likely to make a difference to the outcome it generates. Note that this observation also has the potential to undermine the usefulness for assessing the impact of a potential tax change of a standard cost-benefit analysis, which is likely to rely on elasticities estimated econometrically from market data on prices and quantities. The change in demand that results from a salient new tax may be unlikely to match such an estimate of elasticity. In these circumstances, policy makers might do better to gather evidence via an experiment or trial, perhaps incorporating variation in the salience of the tax.

As with defaults and convenience, policy makers need to consider the importance of salience not only with respect to their own attempts to communicate information, but also with respect to the way providers communicate with consumers. Frequently, policy makers might be concerned about individuals paying insufficient attention to key attributes of products, such as fees, additional price components and penalty rates, or paying too much attention to potentially irrelevant features, such as data on the past performance of financial products where the provider has selected the period over which performance is measured. The empirical studies above show that where the total price of a good is not immediately apparent, there is the potential to manipulate consumer demand. An important point to note here is that competition within a market can, in principle, exacerbate problems related to salience. Gabaix and Laibson (2006) label instances where firms seek to hide certain product attributes or components of the total price as "shrouding". They show how competition in a market may enhance rather than drive out incentives for firms to shroud attributes, exploiting consumers' limited attention and causing consumer detriment, at least for some consumers.

Of particular concern here is partitioned pricing, where price components are separated and, therefore, some components may be more salient than others. This includes "drip pricing", in which components are added to the price as the purchaser proceeds through the purchase process, e.g. by adding handling fees, optional extras, etc. Combining evidence from experiments and consumer surveys, the Office of Fair Trading (2010a) concluded that, of a range of price advertising techniques studied, drip pricing was the form of price advertising most likely to mislead consumers. Findings such as these support the view that regulation may be needed in some markets to force suppliers to disclose the total cost of products up front (Bar-Gill, 2011).

Given that the salience of a piece of information can have a substantial effect on decisions, any regulator seeking to improve decisions might want to consider carefully the various points at which the communication of reliable and helpful information is possible. For instance, in a consumer market for an ordinary shop bought good, unsolicited information that might influence purchase decisions can be supplied through advertising, packaging, labelling, price-tags, or at the till. In the online environment, opportunities to supply useful information are perhaps more tightly constrained to information (or hyperlinks) supplied on the specific website. Where purchase involves a lengthy discussion with a salesperson, such as for financial products, it is possible to mandate written or verbal disclosures. Products that involve ongoing consumer contracts and billing introduce the possibility of mandating feedback or other information on the bill. In each context, there are limited opportunities to engage the consumer. A similar analysis can be applied to regulation in areas such as health and safety, labour market regulation, or compliance with regulations on taxation and environmental standards, and so on. In each case, there are limited opportunities for attracting and holding the attention of the key decision makers concerned. Effective policy will aim to make best use of these opportunities to communicate with decision makers.

A final issue for policy design in relation to the salience of information concerns the potential for unintended consequences. If important information is being ignored, increasing its salience does not guarantee that it will then be appropriately weighted in decisions, nor that incorporating it will not result in inappropriate reweighting of other information. An instructive example concerns an experiment on financial advice carried out for the European Commission (2010). Participants in the experiment had to decide between retail investment products. Those receiving financial advice initially paid too little attention to the possibility that their advisor had a conflict of interest. Yet participants for whom the conflict was made more salient gave the information perhaps too much weight, in that they denied themselves some financially beneficial options that would also have benefited the advisor.

Once it is accepted that decision makers can overweight and/or underweight different information, it is easier to identify a shortcoming in decision making than to improve it unambiguously. As with simplification, defaults and convenience, this means that gauging the effect of a policy may require empirical evidence that is specific to the policy context or intervention.

4.4 Debiasing and decision quality

Even if decision makers possess comprehensible information, face options of equivalent convenience and attend to all appropriate information, there are very many behavioural findings that link certain aspects of the structure of decisions to a greater likelihood of suboptimal outcomes. These effects are often characterised as "biases" and attempts by policy makers to improve biased decision making as "debiasing".

A simple example relates to the research of Larrick and Soll (2008), who revealed a consistent error in the way many consumers process fuel efficiency information presented in terms of miles-per-gallon (MPG). This example and the associated redesign of US fuel efficiency labels is considered in detail in Box 1. A similar case of trying to counteract individuals' tendencies to make linear judgements concerns the effects of compound interest. Evidence relating to financial literacy reveals that a substantial proportion of consumers do not appreciate that interest compounds (e.g. Lusardi, 2010). The result is that they are likely to underestimate the total cost of loans. One potential way to counteract this is to mandate worked examples on credit card bills, mortgage disclosures, loan documentation and so on. For instance, bills and statements can include calculations of the time taken and total interest costs of paying off outstanding loan balances. Annual statements can be mandated that allow consumers to compare more easily the total cost of credit over an extended period. With respect to credit cards, rather than regulating to introduce a mandated annual statement, the UK government has made an agreement with the UK Card Association to introduce annual statements, which detail the total cost of using the card over the preceding 12 months, broken down by types of fees and charges. More empirical research is needed to assess whether this policy and similar mandates contained in the US CARD Act do, in fact, change the behaviour of consumers (see Box 2).

In both of the above cases, there is evidence that a behavioural effect leads to disadvantageous decision making – people struggle to estimate quantities that are changing in a non-linear fashion. More generally, it may not be so easy to identify the extent of detriment, to isolate the cause, and to find an intervention that unambiguously improves outcomes. Notwithstanding the issue of whether the government has a right to regulate to "debias" people's decisions, meeting these conditions can be difficult.

A relevant example relates to energy efficient appliances, where research has consistently shown that consumers buy cheaper but less efficient and ultimately, therefore, more expensive appliances. In this case, provided consumers are not credit constrained, the long-term detriment associated with buying less efficient appliances seems pretty clear. From the point of view of a policy maker who might wish to promote energy efficiency, however, the difficulty is to isolate and to address the cause. Hypotheses range from the excessive complexity of information on energy efficiency, to consumers overweighting of immediate losses in comparison to future gains, to the difficulty of perceiving and hence trusting the gains when weighed up against the certain and easily perceived monetary loss. This example raises a key issue in using behavioural economics in policy design, namely that there is often a range of potentially relevant phenomena.

The cause of detriment may be hard to determine and may not generalise beyond the specific market context.

In many of the examples introduced thus far, it is relatively easy to show that some decision makers are making mistakes. In other words, there is a way to assess the quality of decisions. Fuel efficiency, compound interest and long-term costs of running appliances that perform equivalent tasks are arguably matters of accounting and, consequently, how adept people are at the associated calculations can be studied with some confidence. Policy makers might be willing to assume that people do not have preferences to pay more in return for equivalent quality and, therefore, that any regulations that help to create a market where calculations are more accurate will be welcome, assuming they are not excessively costly to implement. In other circumstances, however, it can be much more difficult to determine whether a mistake is being made.

Notable examples are the future health implications of choices over food, physical activity, tobacco and alcohol. Many individuals wish to change their own patterns of behaviour yet find it hard to make daily decisions consistent with long-term goals. Some might welcome interventions that make it easier to control their own behaviour – environments that make healthy eating or physical exercise more likely, restrictions on the availability of alcohol and tobacco, etc. But determining that any one type of decision represents a mistake, or that decisions made in a particular environment are subject to a disadvantageous bias, is much more difficult. This review does not concern itself with normative debates about the extent to which regulators have any business intervening in such decisions. Nevertheless, even if one accepts that they do, it is often unclear what criteria can be used to assess whether decisions are actually being improved by a given intervention.

Similarly, many important decisions taken by consumers, businesspeople and policy makers involve assessment of risk over the medium to long term. In addition to the body of evidence suggesting that decisions display time inconsistency (see above), there is good evidence that individuals find it hard to process probability and often fail to choose among risky options in a consistent manner (see DellaVigna, 2009, for a recent review). Furthermore, individuals display ambiguity aversion, meaning that they are more inclined to take an equivalent risk when they feel able to assess it, even if erroneously (e.g. Fox and Tversky, 1995). Accumulated evidence suggests that these phenomena affect financial decisions (Barberis and Thaler, 2003), decisions over insurance (Schwarcz, 2010) and choice of telecommunications contracts (Lunn, 2013a).

Behavioural economics offers many explanations for such phenomena and associated avenues for designing policies that might have a positive influence on these decisions. But in these cases it is difficult to determine which decisions are, in fact, detrimental and, if so, to what extent. The scientific results show that revealed preferences (those implied by the choices individuals actually make) are at least sometimes and perhaps often inconsistent, but not which are the optimal decisions and which the suboptimal ones. Thus, when designing policy, revealed preferences cannot be assumed to be normative, i.e. what people choose may not be in their own best interests, yet policy makers may not be able to compare pre-intervention decisions and post-intervention decisions and thereby determine whether the intervention has improved welfare, or whether it has had a redistributive impact by improving the welfare of some consumers but not others (see Lunn, 2013b, for discussion and examples of these problems).

Beshears et al. (2008) list six forms of empirical evidence that, even where revealed preferences cannot be considered normative, might nevertheless give policy makers helpful insight into people's true preferences: active choices made by engaged decision makers; asymptotic choices made by experienced decision makers; aggregated choices across individuals; self-reported preferences; informed choices made by those with expertise or training; and structural estimation, where a model of revealed choices is estimated and mapped onto a normative decision-making framework. Other forms of evidence might be added to these. It may be informative to discover how decision makers respond to feedback regarding how their decisions are affected by variation in the choice-set or by the framing of the decision. For instance, once people have had the inconsistency of their own choices and their susceptibility to a framing effect explained, their response may offer an indication of the desirability of each choice. Such evidence is unlikely to be conclusive, but may be indicative.

4.5 Regulatory method

The many examples described above of how behavioural economics is influencing regulatory design allow some generalisations to be made. This subsection concentrates on three related observations: the difficulty of measuring effect size; some behavioural phenomena that are well documented in both laboratory and field but which, to date, have had less influence on policy design than the phenomena focused on above; and the more empirical approach being adopted by some regulators. It is argued that these observations provide some indication of how the future incorporation of behavioural research into regulatory policy is likely to proceed.

The inductive nature of behavioural economics means that much of the debate about its implications for policy surrounds what can be safely inferred from the very many and varied empirical findings, most of which are experimental. In this regard, the volume of evidence surrounding a range of prominent behavioural phenomena is sufficient to persuade many researchers and policy makers that systematic departures from rational choice theory are common. But it is much easier to infer the likely presence of a particular phenomenon than it is to draw conclusions about its relative importance. That is, the presence of an effect is easier to determine than the size of the effect.

For instance, looking at the available evidence, few would doubt that the complexity of the decisions facing consumers in certain markets can cause detriment, or that consumers sometimes fail to take account of less obvious price components. The presence of these effects, perhaps in quite a large number of markets is, on the balance of probabilities, highly likely. The relevant phenomena have been identified and recorded in the laboratory and in the field. Yet it is very much harder, empirically, to estimate how much detriment is involved. Furthermore, while it is relatively straightforward to devise a policy that ought, in theory, to be helpful for decision makers, it is again much harder to gauge the amount of benefit likely to be gained or whether the intervention may help some consumers yet hinder others. Mandating simplified products is a reasoned response to evidence that complexity of offerings is confusing consumers and undermining competition, but this does not guarantee that the benefits gained will trump the costs of imposing such a measure. Mandating the disclosure of a total cost price is a reasoned response to evidence of consumers choosing more expensive service contracts with apparently hidden costs, but this does not necessarily mean that the contracts concerned will then be outcompeted in the market once this regulation is in place.

The exceptions to this generalisation are themselves instructive. Effect size is much easier to demonstrate when decision makers face a binary decision: to join the pension scheme or not; to be an organ donor or not. In both these cases the demonstrably large effect size associated with changing the default has proved highly persuasive to policy makers in several countries and has led to regulatory policy changes. Furthermore, the claims that we need increased pension provision and more organ donors are, for the most part, uncontroversial. However, most decisions are not binary and often aggregate outcomes are controversial. For instance, consumers may or may not be missing out on very large accumulated surpluses from making poor choices of mortgages, banking services, utilities contracts, mobile and broadband services, and so on. It is not hard to cite behavioural phenomena that are suggestive, especially where revealed preferences can be shown to be inconsistent, but it is very difficult to demonstrate the size of the effects involved. In such markets, where quality is partly subjective, it is hard to determine empirically that the outcome of one choice is superior to another, harder still to determine by how much, and harder again to estimate an aggregated effect size across the market.

Thus, while many researchers and policy makers agree that the findings of behavioural economics have potentially important implications for policy, there is much less agreement about what those ultimate implications are. This helps to explain why the applications of behavioural economics undertaken thus far have been concentrated on simplification, convenience and salience. Although there remains doubt about the size of the benefits such regulations might bring, which may or may not outweigh the costs, the intention to offer assistance to consumers is clear and relatively uncontroversial.

One might contrast this with some of the potential implications of other behavioural findings that have been repeatedly demonstrated in laboratories and in many cases in the field. An example is how individuals intuitively overweight low probabilities. This phenomenon may go some way to explaining why so many people repeatedly lose large sums of money gambling, for seemingly little gain (see, for example, Productivity Commission, 2010). Similarly, the findings imply that people may systematically purchase insurance that they don't need. The losses involved here are potentially very large, but uncertain and extremely difficult to demonstrate. It is a long way to generalise from a laboratory experiment that shows how probabilities are overweighted, when betting a few dollars on the colour of balls drawn from a bingo cage, to the actions of gamblers losing substantial sums playing online poker.

Parallel arguments can easily be generated for the extent of potential consumer detriment when purchasing financial services or trading in asset markets, where perceptions of the level of risk and ambiguity are vital to good decision making. Behavioural findings are suggestive of systematic misperceptions likely to distort investment decisions in these markets, again with the potential for large welfare losses. However, while such effects might again be demonstrable in a laboratory, they are very hard to test for and estimate empirically in the key markets concerned.

The difficulty of estimating effect sizes and generalising scientific findings to highly specific market contexts helps to explain aspects of the regulatory approach being taken in many cases where behavioural findings are influencing policy. Both factors imply a great degree of uncertainty in translating behavioural phenomena into concrete regulations or other policy actions. Consequently, there is a strong argument for incorporating the inductive scientific method into policy making itself. In other words, the difficulty of estimating effect sizes and concerns about the translation of findings across contexts means that policy makers might do well to conduct or commission context specific testing of their interventions.

Indeed, many of the institutions and agencies that have begun to pursue behavioural policy agendas are taking a more empirical approach to policy design. OIRA has encouraged US federal agencies to undertake empirical analyses of their regulations. The CFPB has carried out pretesting of its proposed simplified disclosures intended to underpin its "know before you owe" initiative in the mortgage, credit card and student loan markets. UKBIT has made the empirical testing of innovative behavioural policy designs central to its methods and has sought to extend the approach to other areas of the public service by publishing a guide (*Test, Learn, Adapt*) on how to conduct of RCTs, experiments and trials to improve policy design (Behavioural Insights Team, 2012b).

The crux of this argument is the recognition that this approach is a natural extension of the inductive scientific method that has characterised the rise to prominence of behavioural economics. The method is perhaps necessary given the complex and multi-faceted nature of economic decision making. A notable consequence of this more inductive approach to policy development is that it marks a further significant departure from the use of neoclassical economics to inform policy, which has traditionally relied upon highly generalised and powerful deductive models. Instead, the behavioural approach implies caution when generalising models from one policy domain to another. Its findings suggest hypotheses and policies worth testing and trialling, while its scientific approach offers methods to undertake the necessary empirical work. The result is a much more empirical approach to regulation.

A more empirical approach to regulatory policy can also have an upside in terms of providing confidence in the objectivity and impartiality of the regulatory process (cf. OECD, 2012, Recommendation 7). Empirical findings can be made available and, where appropriate, contribute to the scientific process. Consumers and businesses can be more confident of the objectivity and impartiality of a regulator who designs and amends proposals in response not to lobbying, politics or ideology, but to published empirical results.

5. Regulatory delivery

The concept of regulatory delivery refers not to the design of regulations but to the way in which regulation is conducted. This covers aspects of the institutional architecture, such as the number and nature of the regulators, and also how they go about the task of ensuring compliance with the regulations for which they are responsible. The increased emphasis on regulatory delivery in recent years (see, for example, Local Better Regulation Office, 2012) is built on the insight that how regulations are implemented can have an important influence on business activity and, ultimately, growth. Regulatory delivery can affect costs, efficiency and the likelihood that businesses comply with regulations designed to produce economic, social and environmental outcomes.

This shorter section briefly examines some of the potential implications of behavioural economics for regulatory delivery. This is less well-worn territory than the material covered in preceding sections and, consequently, the analysis is more forward-looking and speculative. Nevertheless, it is concluded that the influence of behavioural economics on regulatory delivery is likely to grow. The primary reason for this is that although little behavioural research has thus far addressed the issue of regulatory delivery, established principles of behavioural economics are of clear relevance.

The distinction between regulatory design and delivery, while helpful, is not in fact all that clean. The reason for this is that it is generally the regulators tasked with implementing regulations who determine priorities for enforcement and who monitor how well regulations are working. This argument parallels one repeatedly made with respect to the unclean distinction between policy and policy implementation; "street level bureaucrats" do not merely implement, they create (Lipsky, 1980). Part of good regulatory delivery must be to provide some flexibility and feedback with respect to how regulations operate on the ground. This is necessary for improving the efficiency of the regulatory system concerned – good regulatory delivery interacts with regulatory design.

With this in mind, it is instructive to reconsider the conclusions drawn in Section 4 about the need to take a more empirical approach to regulation. It is an oft-cited criticism of behavioural economics that it is likely to lead to excessive intervention in markets. Yet a moment's reflection on the scientific findings associated with simplification, convenience and salience, would suggest that many existing regulations may themselves be too complex and cumbersome to be effective. Behavioural economics provides empirical methodologies for designing experiments to test old regulations for effectiveness. Indeed, for this reason, in 2011, OIRA required US federal regulators to put in place strategies for retrospective empirical tests of existing regulations. Thus, a behavioural economic approach suggests that part of good regulatory delivery is to conduct ongoing empirical analysis of the effectiveness of present regulations, to provide necessary evidence to remove ineffective yet burdensome regulation (cf. OECD, 2012, Recommendation 5). Research detailing where and how this has been done effectively would be of benefit.

Although less behavioural work has examined decision making by firms, there is good reason to believe that at least some findings relating to individual decision making will also apply to the decisions of firms (Armstrong and Huck, 2010). Findings relating to simplification, convenience and salience may hence be relevant to decisions taken by firms in respect of regulatory compliance. The behavioural principle here is straightforward: if it is made easier to comply, then compliance will become more likely.

Simplification lies at the heart of the US "fillable fileable" initiative, which seeks to simplify administrative processes by making greater use of simplified electronic and online forms, often where basic informational fields are pre-populated. The aim is to reduce the burden on business and administration systems. Sunstein (2011) cites a list of 72 administrative changes that flowed from the "fillable fileable" initiative. Using such methods to reduce the burden of paperwork and form-filling for businesses is an obvious route to better regulatory delivery (Hampton, 2005).

Consideration of the idea that convenient options are more attractive implies that the immediate inconvenience of compliance may be a frequent reason for breaching regulations. Cutting corners, perhaps with respect to health and safety, environmental protection, food hygiene and so on, is in effect the triumph of immediate convenience over longer-term risks and/or benefits. This suggests that good regulatory delivery involves not just enforcement, but also providing assistance to businesses to set up convenient yet compliant systems. Inspectors often possess expertise that businesses do not, placing them in a good position to work with firms in order to achieve this.

A potentially important behavioural principle here relates to how individual behaviour is influenced by perceptions of fairness. Two aspects, both established by extensive scientific literatures, may be relevant to compliance. First, people are capable of acting against their own financial interests where they perceive unfairness. Hence, where individuals or organisations feel unfairly treated by authorities, they may be more inclined to risk negative consequences through non-cooperation. Second, most individuals are generally willing to incur costs for the greater good provided they are confident that others are doing the same. These responses to perceived fairness suggest that the treatment of firms by regulators and their knowledge of how other firms behave are likely to influence compliance. The importance of maintaining trust of the regulated by regulators is an important principle in the governance of regulators (OECD, 2013b).

Work carried out in a number of countries on tax compliance is of relevance here. UKBIT, in collaboration with the United Kingdom's tax authorities, has undertaken a series of RCTs designed to assess the impact of different forms of communication on compliance (Behavioural Insights Team, 2012). The RCTs involve varying the contents of letters sent to noncompliant individuals and businesses and have thus far been used to study the effectiveness of different communications in the collection of late self-assessed income tax; arrears from non-compliant medical practices; unpaid company taxation, tax from non-compliant sole traders; overpaid tax credits; and unwarranted single-person discounts for local taxation. In general, tax compliance is increased by communications designed to make it easy to pay and by providing information on the proportion of taxpayers in the local area who have paid their tax (in places where compliance is high). These experiments are a good example of where the empirical approach to regulation can increase efficiency and save substantial sums on costly enforcement actions.

As highlighted in previous sections, the biggest inroads into policy made by behavioural economics have been in consumer and competition policy. Regulatory delivery in these areas frequently involves market studies designed to assess the extent, if any, of consumer detriment and to design and potentially test remedies. Section 3 described how in various countries consumer and competition authorities have begun to recruit or train staff to increase their expertise in behavioural economics. This suggests that skills in behavioural economics are increasingly being recognised as important to regulatory delivery in this area.

The recent changes in financial regulation in the United States and United Kingdom following the financial crisis provide good examples. Both new agencies, the CFPB and the FCA respectively have recruited behavioural economists. These regulators have recognised that where their own staff are in the process of supervising a firm, investigating a potential breach of regulations, or considering the potential for a particular product or marketing technique to cause consumer detriment, knowledge of the established phenomena of behavioural economics is likely to be of assistance in understanding observed behaviour and forming judgements.

That is, in many instances, the application of behavioural economics to policy occurs not only at the level of regulatory design, but also at the stage of regulatory delivery, when the existing rules and regulations are interpreted and enforced.

An interesting issue here is the extent to which engagement with ongoing research can contribute to regulatory delivery. In this context, it is worth noting the role of behavioural economics in the work of the Office of Fair Trading (OFT) in the United Kingdom, which was arguably an early adopter of some behavioural thinking. The OFT has carried out or commissioned a series of influential behavioural studies, including on the degree to which consumers' decision making is affected by how prices are framed and advertised (Office of Fair Trading, 2010a, 2010b). The insights in these reports would be of clear use to OFT analysts wishing to assess the degree of effective competition and consumer protection within a given market setting.

In the United States, the CFPB has also sought to engage financial services providers with ongoing research into how consumers respond to information disclosure. "Project Catalyst", announced in November 2012, invites providers to contribute to empirically informed regulation by trialling new forms of disclosure or other innovations aimed at improving consumers' decision making. The research will be conducted in collaboration with the regulator.

In sum, the examples in this section show how behavioural economics is having an impact on regulatory delivery in a number of areas, perhaps notably those where it is also having the biggest influence on regulatory design. While there are presently fewer examples to draw lessons from and less available research in comparison to regulatory design, there may be considerable scope for employing principles derived from behavioural economics to improve regulatory delivery.

6. Conclusions

The findings of behavioural economics are increasingly being used to inform policy in many countries. While the United States and the United Kingdom have pioneered the explicit application of behavioural economics to policy, a number of other countries have also begun to adopt behaviourally informed approaches. The European Commission is employing behavioural research in policy design. Among others, Australia, France, Denmark, Sweden and Norway have identifiable initiatives aimed at promoting behavioural thinking among policy makers. Such initiatives are also likely to result in implicit applications of behavioural insights to policy making that may not be documented and studied to the same extent, but may nevertheless represent important contributions to policy.

Although behavioural economics has many potential applications to service delivery and redistributive policy, a large proportion of the policy applications of behavioural economics thus far relates to regulatory policy, defined broadly to encompass potential alternatives to regulation. Most of these developments have occurred within the last five years. The spread of behavioural economics in policy making has therefore been rapid and wide.

Consumer and competition policy are the areas in which behaviourally informed thinking is making the biggest strides. The most common applications involve mandating or supplying information in order to simplify the decisions that economic actors face, to make better options more convenient, or to increase the salience of key information. Other important applications include the setting of beneficial defaults, especially with respect to pension policy, and various attempts to "debias" economic actors where empirical evidence suggests systematically disadvantageous decision making.

While scientific evidence lies behind many of these behaviourally informed policies, the size of the effects concerned and thus the likely outcomes of interventions based on them are difficult to measure and to estimate for the specific market context in which an intervention is proposed or introduced. Behavioural economic studies often reveal subtle and complex influences on decision making, where large effects are demonstrable but precise causal mechanisms have not unambiguously been identified. Thus, the extent to which an effect translates to a given policy context may be unclear. Many interventions, therefore, are based on sound empirical findings, but depend for effectiveness upon uncertain effect sizes, meaning that likely policy impacts are hard to assess.

This in an important issue for policy. It suggests that careful attention needs to be paid to the extent to which an effect can be assumed to operate within a specific market context. Regarding the broader approach to policy development, it implies that there may be benefits to policy makers adopting the more inductive approach to economic analysis that lies at the heart of behavioural economics. This entails policy makers and regulators being prepared to undertake or commission context-specific empirical studies that employ experiments, pilots and RCTs. In those countries that are pioneering behavioural applications to policy, the use of such empirical approaches is expanding and could compliment traditional regulatory policy tools such as regulatory impact assessments.

This conclusion has implications for applied economic analysis and the skill-sets of those working in policy development and regulation. Cost-benefit analyses and regulatory impact assessments are resource intensive exercises, designed to gather the available evidence, place it into a sound theoretical framework, and thus produce a reliable estimate regarding the merits of a specific intervention. Once such an exercise has been conducted, the answer it provides is meant to endure, at least over the medium term. Contrastingly, the behavioural approach involves a much more dynamic interface between evidence, theory and policy. The large array of available behavioural findings may be used to generate multiple ideas for improving the decision making of economic actors in different contexts. But whether the effect on which an intervention is based generalises to the specific context will be an empirical question. Results in analogous contexts may act as a good guide to which initiatives are worth considering, but reliable estimates of the likely impact will probably require one or more empirical studies within the specific market concerned. Conducting such studies requires different scientific skills to the deductive analytic exercises more traditionally associated with good regulatory policy, with implications for training, recruitment and, perhaps, the relationship between academic researchers and policy makers.

Advances in behavioural economics throw up another challenge to policy makers. The orthodox assumption of stable preferences is now questioned by numerous findings that record apparently inconsistent preferences. Thus, to a presently unknown extent, revealed preferences are an imperfect guide to individuals' best interests. The upshot is that in markets where such effects can be observed, it is very difficult for policy makers to make a sound assessment of any potential detriment and to determine that an intervention will lead to an unambiguous improvement in outcomes.

This conclusion is consistent with the observation that the earliest examples where behavioural economics has been applied to policy mostly involve changing the way information is communicated, with a focus on simplification, convenience and salience – for improving both regulatory design and regulatory delivery. Such regulatory measures are likely to prove popular with consumers and are, relatively speaking, uncontentious, since they aim to reduce the likelihood of consumers making clearly identifiable decision errors – failing to understand or notice something of importance. Yet many other behavioural findings lead to much more contentious issues regarding the quality of decision making. Are individuals who spend sizeable proportions of income gambling, or who invest in risky assets, or who engage in activities likely to cause themselves long-term harm, making mistakes?

This review has largely focussed on positive rather than normative analysis – how *is* behavioural economics being applied, not how *should* it be applied. Yet the distinction is not entirely clean. The applications of behavioural economics undertaken thus far have tended to concentrate on interventions and markets where it is most apparent that decision makers are not acting in their own best interests, or at least not their own financial interests. There are many markets, however, where it is possible that behavioural phenomena play an important part, where poor decisions may be very costly, but where it is presently unclear how to identify disadvantageous decisions and the extent of the disadvantage involved. Such issues may, or may not, prove amenable to empirical analysis.

The last section considered the potential application of behavioural economics to regulatory delivery, i.e. the implementation of regulations. It identified instances where behavioural principles can be used to limit regulatory burdens. This might involve the ongoing testing of existing regulations, making compliance easier, prioritising fair implementation and testing the effectiveness of communications with regulated entities. As with regulatory design, a behavioural approach to regulatory delivery has implications for the skills required of regulators.

A final, more general point is worth making here. While this review has focussed on specific examples of how behavioural economics is being applied to regulatory design or regulatory delivery, it may be having a more general impact on regulatory policy as a whole. Behavioural economics shows how behaviour is influenced by much more than rules and the enforcement of rules. It reveals how much the environment in which decision makers operate matters. Regulations are just one possible way to alter that environment, but where they are effective it may often be less because they prohibit than because they assist; good regulations can improve the environment for decision makers. Thus, behavioural economics may be affecting the fundamental attitude of governments toward regulation, helping to reinforce the idea of regulation not as merely a constraint on behaviour but as an enabler and a facilitator to achieve positive outcomes.

From the position of a sometimes marginalised subdiscipline, behavioural economics has been swept into the mainstream with surprising speed. This review has aimed to document part of this process and to consider the implications. Perhaps the broadest conclusion that can be drawn is that as well as suggesting some potential answers for policy makers, behavioural economics is continuing to raise important questions about what policy can and cannot do to assist us all to make better decisions.

Bibliography

Agnew, J.R. and Szykman, L.R. (2005), "Asset Allocation and Information Overload: The Influence of Information Display, Asset Choice, and Investor Experience", *Journal of Behavioral Finance*, 6: 57–70.

Agarwal, S. et al. (2013), "Regulating Consumer Financial Products: Evidence from Credit Cards", *NBER Working Paper No. 19484.*

Allcott, H. (2013), "The Welfare Effects of Misperceived Product Costs: Data and Calibrations from the Automobile Market", *American Economic Journal: Economic Policy*, 5: 30-66.

Armstrong, M. and Huck, S. (2010), "Behavioural Economics as Applied to Firms: a Primer", *Competition Policy International*, 6: 3-45.

Barberis, N. and Thaler, R. (2003), "A Survey of Behavioral Finance", In *Handbook of the Economics of Finance*, Constantinides, G.M., Harris, M. and Stulz, R. (eds.), Elsevier Science.

Bar-Gill, O. (2011), "Competition and Consumer protection: A Behavioral Economics Account", *Law and Economics Research Paper Series, Working Paper No. 11-42*, New York University School of Law.

Behavioural Insights Team (2011), *Annual Update 2010-2011*, Cabinet Office, London.

Behavioural Insights Team (2012a), *Applying Behavioural Insights to Reduce Fraud, Error and Debt*, Cabinet Office, London.

Behavioural Insights Team (2012b), *Test, Learn, Adapt*, Cabinet Office, London.

Bertrand, M. et al. (2010), "What's Advertising Content Worth? Evidence from a Consumer Credit Marketing Field Experiment", *Quarterly Journal of Economics*, 125: 263-306.

Beshears, J. et al. (2008), "How are Preferences Revealed?", *Journal of Public Economics*, 92: 1787-1794.

Beshears. J. et al. (2010), "How Does Simplified Disclosure Affect Individuals' Mutual Fund Choices?" *NBER Working Paper No. 14859.*

Bettinger, E.P. et al. (2009), "The Role of Simplification and Information in College Decisions: Results from the H&R Block FAFSA Experiment", *NBER Working Paper No. 15361*.

Carroll, G.D. et al. (2009), "Optimal Defaults and Active Decisions", *Quarterly Journal of Economics*, 124: 1639-1674.

Centre d'analyse stratégique (2010), *Improving Public Health Prevention with Behavioural, Cognitive and Neuroscience*, Premier Ministre, Paris.

Centre d'analyse stratégique (2011), *Green Nudges: New Incentives for Ecological Behaviour*, Premier Ministre, Paris.

Chetty, R., A. Looney and K. Kroft (2009), "Salience and Taxation: Theory and Evidence", *American Economic Review*, 99: 1145-1177.

Congdon, W.J., J.R. Kling, and S.Mullainathan (2011), *Policy and Choice: Public Finance Through the Lens of Behavioural Economics*, Brookings Institution Press, Washington DC.

Cooper, J. et al. (2010), "Super System Review Final Report, Part One, Overview and Recommendations", www.SuperSystemReview.gov.au.

DellaVigna, S. (2009), "Psychology and Economics: Evidence from the Field", *Journal of Economic Literature,* 47: 315-372.

Department for Business, Innovation and Skills (2011), *Better Choices, Better Deals: Consumers Powering Growth*. Department for Business, Innovation and Skills/Cabinet Office, London.

Department of Health (2008). *Consultation on the Future of Tobacco Control*. Department of Health, London.

Department of Finance and Deregulation (2012), *Influencing Consumer Behaviour: Improving Regulatory Design*, Department of Finance and Deregulation, Canberra.

Dolan, P. et al. (2010), "MINDSPACE: Influencing Behaviour Through Public Policy". The Cabinet Office/Institute for Government, London.

Erta, K. et al. (2013), "Applying Behavioural Economics at the Financial Conduct Authority", *Occasional Paper No. 1*, Financial Conduct Authority, London.

European Commission (2010), *Consumer Decision-Making in Retail Investment Services: A Behavioural Economics Perspective*, European Commission, Brussels.

Fox, C.R. and A. Tversky (1995), "Ambiguity Aversion and Comparative Ignorance", *Quarterly Journal of Economics*, 110: 585-603.

Frederick, S., G. Loewenstein, and T. O'Donoghue (2002), "Time Discounting and Time Preference: A Critical Review", *Journal of Economic Literature*, 40: 351-401.

Gabaix, X. and D. Laibson (2006), "Shrouded Attributes and Information Suppression in Competitive Markets", *Quarterly Journal of Economics*, 121: 505-540.

Garcés, E. (2010), "The Impact of Behavioral Economics on Consumer and Competition Policies", *Competition Policy International*, 6: 145-152.

Garner, R. (2005), "Post-It® Note Persuasion: A Sticky Influence", *Journal of Consumer Psychology*, 15: 230–7.

Giulietti, M., C. Waddams Price, and M. Waterson (2005), "Consumer Choice and Competition Policy: a Study of UK Energy Markets", *Economic Journal*, 115: 949-968.

Hampton, P. (2005), *Reducing Administrative Burdens: Effective Inspection and Enforcement*, HM Treasury, London.

Hossain, T. and J. Morgan (2006). "...Plus Shipping and Handling: Revenue (Non)- Equivalence in Field Experiments on eBay", *B.E. Journals in Economic Analysis and Policy: Advances in Economic Analysis and Policy*, 6: 1-27.

House of Lords Science and Technology Committee (2011), "Behaviour Change", www.parliament.uk/hlbehaviour.

Iyengar, S.S., G. Huberman, and W. Jiang (2004), "How Much Choice Is Too Much? Contributions to 401(k) Retirement Plans", In *Pension Design and Structure: New Lessons from Behavioral Finance*, Mitchell, O.S and Steve Utkus, S. (eds.). Oxford University Press, Oxford.

Iyengar, S.S. and E. Kamenica (2010), "Choice Proliferation, Simplicity Seeking, and Asset Allocation", *Journal of Public Economics*, 94: 530-539.

Iyengar, S. and M. Lepper (2000), "When Choice is Demotivating: Can One Desire Too Much of a Good Thing?" *Journal of Personality and Social Psychology*, 79: 995-1006.

Johnson, E. J. and D. Goldstein (2003), Do Defaults Save Lives? *Science*, 302: 1338-1339.

Kahneman, D. (2011), *Thinking, Fast and Slow*, Penguin, New York and London.

Kahneman, D. (2013), Foreword, in *The Behavioural Foundations of Public Policy*. Shafir, E. (ed.), Princeton University Press, Princeton.

KallBekken, S., S. Håkon, and E.A.T. Hermansen (2013), "Bridging the Energy Efficiency Gap: A Field Experiment on Lifetime Energy Costs and Household Appliances", *Journal of Consumer Policy*, 36: 1-16.

Larrick, R.P. and J.B. Soll (2008), "The MPG Illusion", *Science*, 320: 1593-1594.

Lipsky, M. (1980), *Street-level Bureaucracy: Dilemmas of the Individual in Public Services*, Russell Sage Foundation, New York.

Local Better Regulation Office (2012), "Regulation and Growth", www.bis.gov.uk/brdo/publications, Better Regulatory Delivery Office, London.

Lowi, T.J. (1972), "Four Systems of Policy, Politics, and Choice", *Public Administration Review*, 32: 298-310.

Lunn, P.D. (2012), "Behavioural Economics and Policy making: Learning from the Early Adopters", *Economic and Social Review*, 43: 423-449.

Lunn, P.D. (2013a), "Telecommunications Consumers: A Behavioral Economic Analysis", *Journal of Consumer Affairs*, 47: 167-189.

Lunn, P.D. (2013b), "Are Consumer Decision-Making Phenomena a Fourth Market Failure?", *ESRI Working Paper 455*.

Lusardi, A. (2010), "Americans' Financial Capability", Report Prepared for the Financial Crisis Inquiry Commission, 26 February 2010.

Madrian, B.C. and D.F. Shea (2001), "The Power of Suggestion: Inertia in 401(k) Participation and Savings Behaviour", *Quarterly Journal of Economics*, 116: 1149-1187.

Marzilli Ericson, K.M. and A. Starc (2013), "How Product Standardization Affects Choice: Evidence from the Massachusetts Health Insurance Exchange", *NBER Working Paper No. 19527*.

Micklitz, H-W., L. A. Reisch, and K. Hagen (2011), "An Introduction to the Special Issue on 'Behavioural Economics, Consumer Policy and the Law'", *Journal of Consumer Policy*, 34: 271-276.

Monteiro, N. and R. Zaidi (2007), *Market Impacts of MCOB*. Financial Services Authority, London.

Office of Fair Trading (2010a), *Advertising of Prices*, Office of Fair Trading, London.

Office of Fair Trading (2010b), *The Impact of Price Frames on Consumer Decision Making*, Office of Fair Trading, London.

OECD (2012), *Recommendation of the Council on Regulatory Policy and Governance,* www.oecd.org/gov/regulatory-policy/2012recommendation.htm.

OECD (2013a), "Review of the Irish Pension System", www.welfare.ie/en/Pages/Pension-Policy.aspx.

OECD (2013b), "OECD Best Practice Principles for the Governance of Regulators", OECD.

OFGEM (2011), *What Can Behavioural Economics Say About GB Energy Consumers?* OFGEM, London.

OFGEM (2012), *The Retail Market Review – Updated Domestic Proposals.* OFGEM, London.

Productivity Commission (2008a), "Behavioural Economics and Public Policy", Roundtable Proceedings, Productivity Commission, Canberra.

Productivity Commission (2008b), "Review of Australia's Consumer Policy Framework", Final Report, Productivity Commission, Canberra.

Productivity Commission (2010), "Gambling", Report No. 50, Productivity Commission, Canberra.

Rabin, M. (1998), "Psychology and Economics", *Journal of Economic Literature*, 36: 11-46.

Rafaat, R. M., N. Chater, and C. Frith (2009), "Herding in Humans", *Trends in Cognitive Science*, 13: 420–428.

Rick, S.I. (2011), "Losses, Gains, and Brains: Neuroeconomics Can Help to Answer Open Questions about Loss Aversion", *Journal of Consumer Psychology*, 21: 453-463.

Sapsford, D., S.L. Phythian-Adams, and E. Apps (2009), "Behavioural Economics: A Review of the Literature and Proposals for Further Research in the Context of Workplace Health and Safety", *Health and Safety Executive Research Report 752*, Health and Safety Executive, Liverpool.

Scheibehenne, B., R. Greifeneder and P.M. Todd (2010), "Can There Ever Be Too Many Options? A Meta-Analytic Review of Choice Overload", *Journal of Consumer Policy*, 37: 409-425.

Schwarcz, D. (2010), "Insurance Demand Anomalies and Regulation", *Journal of Consumer Affairs*, 44: 557-577.

Shafir, E. (2013), ed., *The Behavioural Foundations of Public Policy,* Princeton University Press, Princeton.

Shiller, R.J. (2005), "Behavioral Economics and Institutional Innovation", *Cowles Foundation Discussion Paper No. 1499*, Yale University.

Shogren, J. (2012), "Behavioural Economics and Environmental Incentives, *OECD Environment Working Papers*, No. 49, OECD Publishing, http://dx.doi.org/10.1787/5k8zwbhqs1xn-en.

Smith, N.C., D.G. Goldstein, and E.J. Johnson (2010), "Smart Defaults: From Hidden Persuaders to Adaptive Helpers", *INSEAD Working Paper No. 2009/03/ISIC*.

Stucke, M.E. (2012), "The Implications of Behavioural Antitrust", Paper prepared for the OECD Directorate for Financial and Enterprise Affairs, Competition Committee, Hearing on Competition and Behavioural Economics, 25 July, 2012.

Sugden, R. (2011), "The Behavioural Economist and the Social Planner: To Whom Should Behavioural Welfare Economics be Addressed?" *Paper on Economics and Evolution No. 1121*, Max Plank Institute of Economics.

Sunstein, C.R. (2011), "Empirically Informed Regulation", *University of Chicago Law Review*, 78: 1348-1429.

Thaler, R. H. and C. R. Sunstein (2003), "Libertarian Paternalism", *American Economic Review*, 93: 175-179.

Thaler, R. H. and S. Benartzi (2004), "Save More Tomorrow: Using Behavioral Economics to Increase Employee Saving", *Journal of Political Economy*, 112: S164-S187.

Thaler, R. H. and S. Mullainathan (2000), "Behavioral Economics", entry in the *International Encyclopedia of the Social and Behavioral Sciences*.

Thaler, R. H. and C. R. Sunstein (2008), *Nudge: Improving Decisions About Health, Wealth, and Happiness*, Yale: Yale University Press.

Tufano, P. (2011), "Just Keep My Money! Supporting Tax-Time Savings with US Savings Bonds", *American Economic Journal: Economic Policy*, 3: 172-200.

US government (2013), "Strengthening Federal Capacity for Behavioral Insights", unpublished document.

Van Bavel, R. et al. (2013), *Applying Behavioural Sciences to EU Policy-*making, Publications Office of the European Union, Luxembourg.

Wilson, C.M. and C. Waddams Price (2010), "Do Consumers Switch to the Best Supplier?", *Oxford Economic Papers*, 62: 647–668.

ORGANISATION FOR ECONOMIC CO-OPERATION AND DEVELOPMENT

The OECD is a unique forum where governments work together to address the economic, social and environmental challenges of globalisation. The OECD is also at the forefront of efforts to understand and to help governments respond to new developments and concerns, such as corporate governance, the information economy and the challenges of an ageing population. The Organisation provides a setting where governments can compare policy experiences, seek answers to common problems, identify good practice and work to co-ordinate domestic and international policies.

The OECD member countries are: Australia, Austria, Belgium, Canada, Chile, the Czech Republic, Denmark, Estonia, Finland, France, Germany, Greece, Hungary, Iceland, Ireland, Israel, Italy, Japan, Korea, Luxembourg, Mexico, the Netherlands, New Zealand, Norway, Poland, Portugal, the Slovak Republic, Slovenia, Spain, Sweden, Switzerland, Turkey, the United Kingdom and the United States. The European Union takes part in the work of the OECD.

OECD Publishing disseminates widely the results of the Organisation's statistics gathering and research on economic, social and environmental issues, as well as the conventions, guidelines and standards agreed by its members.

OECD PUBLISHING, 2, rue André-Pascal, 75775 PARIS CEDEX 16
(42 2014 01 1 P) ISBN 978-92-64-20784-4 – No. 61147 2013-01

Lightning Source UK Ltd.
Milton Keynes UK
UKOW04f1958300115

245431UK00003B/157/P

9 789264 207844